SOUTHWARK:

A walk through time with th

By Shirley Harrison
and Sally Evemy

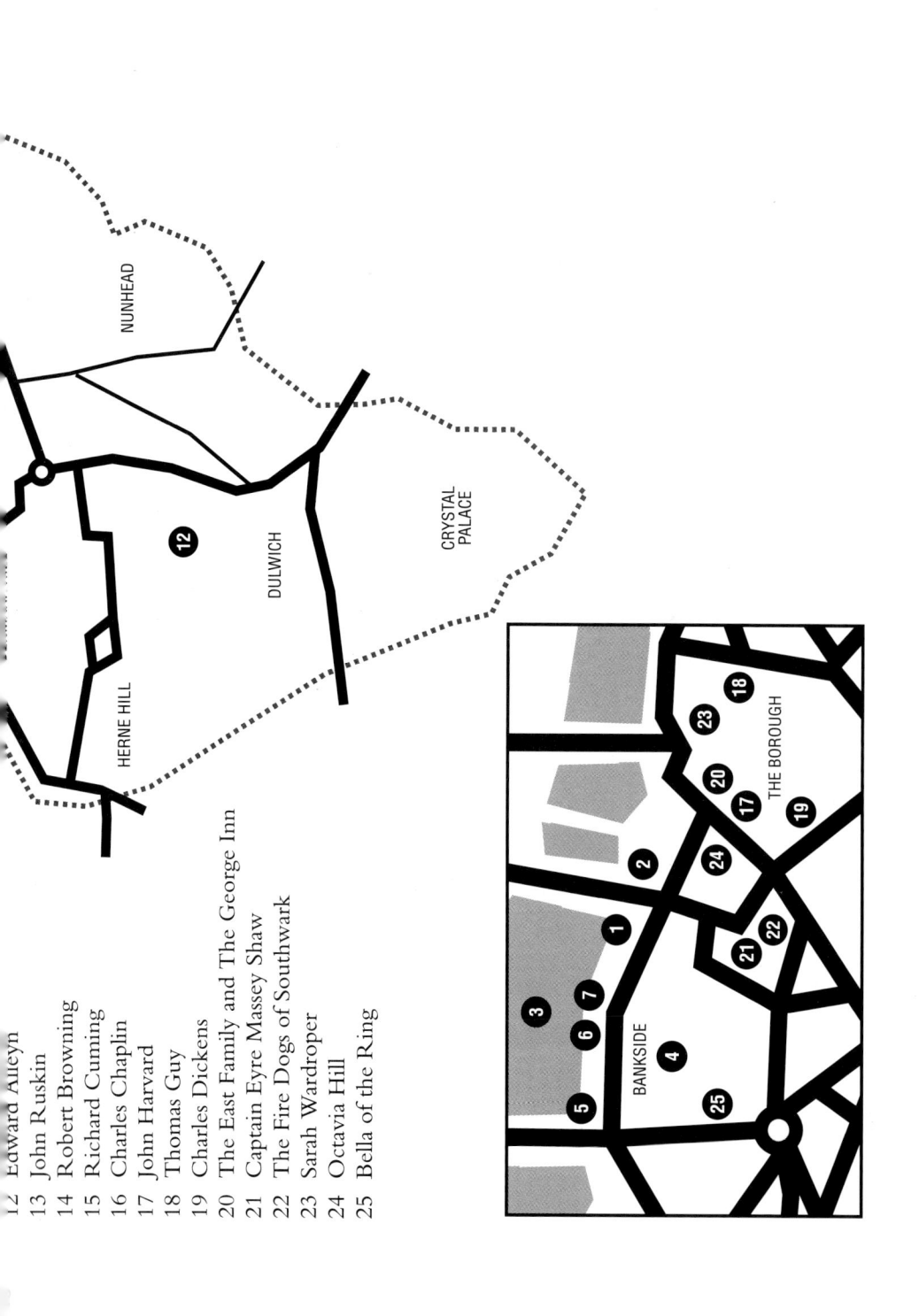

12 Edward Alleyn
13 John Ruskin
14 Robert Browning
15 Richard Cuming
16 Charles Chaplin
17 John Harvard
18 Thomas Guy
19 Charles Dickens
20 The East Family and The George Inn
21 Captain Eyre Massey Shaw
22 The Fire Dogs of Southwark
23 Sarah Wardroper
24 Octavia Hill
25 Bella of the Ring

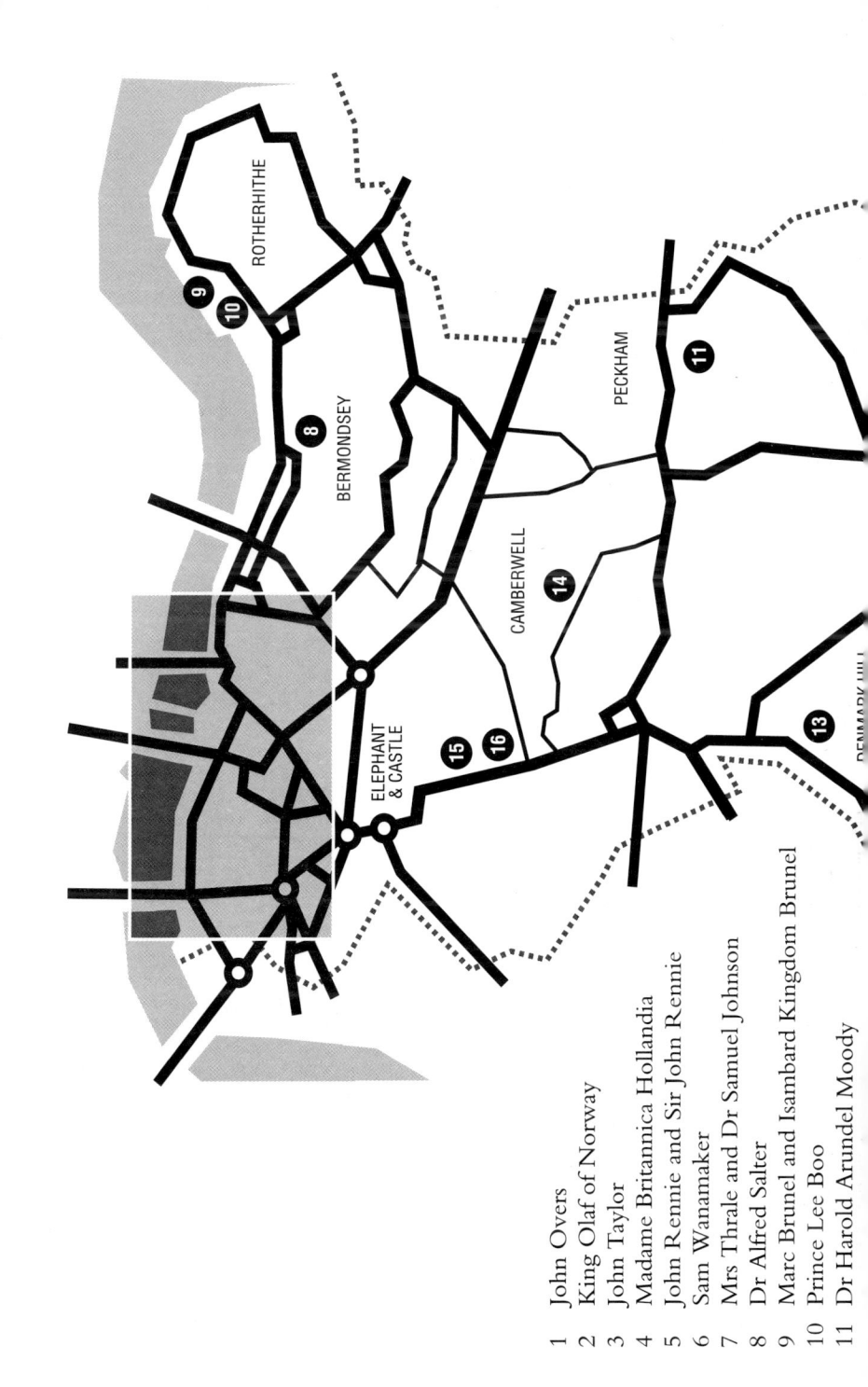

1 John Overs
2 King Olaf of Norway
3 John Taylor
4 Madame Britannica Hollandia
5 John Rennie and Sir John Rennie
6 Sam Wanamaker
7 Mrs Thrale and Dr Samuel Johnson
8 Dr Alfred Salter
9 Marc Brunel and Isambard Kingdom Brunel
10 Prince Lee Boo
11 Dr Harold Arundel Moody

London Borough of Southwark, 2001
Published 2001
© text: Shirley Harrison and Sally Evemy
© London Borough of Southwark

ISBN 0 905849 32 9
British Library Cataloguing in Publication data
A catalogue record for this book is available from the British Library

No part of this publication may be reproduced, stored in a retrieval system or transmitted by any means without prior permission of the Head of Arts, Libraries and Museums.

CONTENTS

Acknowledgements
Introduction   1

ALONG THE RIVER:
BANKSIDE, BERMONDSEY AND ROTHERHITHE
John Overs   8
King Olaf of Norway   10
John Taylor   13
Madame Britannica Hollandia   16
John Rennie and Sir John Rennie   20
Sam Wanamaker   24
Mrs Thrale and Dr Samuel Johnson   28
Dr Alfred Salter   31
Sir Marc Brunel and Isambard Kingdom Brunel   36
Prince Lee Boo   40

SOUTH TO PECKHAM, DULWICH AND CAMBERWELL
Dr Harold Arundel Moody   44
Edward Alleyn   48
John Ruskin   52
Robert Browning   56

ELEPHANT AND CASTLE
AND AROUND THE BOROUGH
Richard Cuming   60
Charles Chaplin   62
John Harvard   66
Thomas Guy   69
Charles Dickens   72
The East Family and The George Inn   75
Captain Eyre Massey Shaw   80
The Fire Dogs of Southwark   84
Sarah Wardroper   87
Octavia Hill   90
Bella of the Ring   93

Booklist   97
Index   100

ACKNOWLEDGEMENTS
We are grateful to Len Reilly, Stephen Humphrey and the staff of Southwark Local Studies Library for sharing their knowledge – and their time. Carol Enright for her design flair. The Florence Nightingale Museum, 2 Lambeth Palace Road, SE1 7EW, for their time and information. John M East for allowing us access to the East family archives and his new book *East of Bedlam*.

We thank the following for the use of their images: Duncan Field, p.4; the Random House Group, p.28; the National Portrait Gallery, p.36; Professor David Killingray, p.44; the Charitable Foundation of Guy's and St Thomas', p.70; John East, p.76, p.77; the London Fire Brigade, p.81, p.84, p.85; Guild of St George Collection, Sheffield Galleries Museums Trust, p.91 and front cover. We apologise if we have failed to gain permission for the reproduction of any images; where possible we have attempted to contact right's holders.

Inside front cover: Southwark Bridge, 1836.
Inside back cover: The Brunel's Thames Tunnel, c.1843.

INTRODUCTION

IT HAPPENED IN THAT SEASON THAT ONE DAY IN SOUTHWARK, AT *The* TABARD AS I LAY READY TO GO ON PILGRIMAGE AND START FOR CANTERBURY, MOST DEVOUT OF HEART SOME NINE AND TWENTY IN A COMPANY OF SUNDRY FOLK HAPPENING THEN TO FALL IN FELLOWSHIP, AND "THEY WERE PILGRIMS ALL…"

One evening in April 1386 a merry band of pilgrims gathered at Southwark's Tabard Inn, on their way to the tomb of Thomas à Becket in Canterbury. Among the company was Geoffrey Chaucer, son of a vintner and now, married to one of Queen Philippa's maids, well placed in the service of King Edward III.

Mellowed as they all were by "nappy ale", the cheerful company responded with enthusiasm to an idea from their genial landlord, Harry Bailly, he suggested they should entertain each other with stories. It was the idea that later inspired Chaucer to write the poem which has brought pilgrims to Southwark and to Canterbury ever since: *The Canterbury Tales*.

Geoffrey Chaucer was born in about 1340, across the river in the City of London. He became a page to King Edward III's daughter-in-law and then valet to the King himself. Eventually, as ambassador, he spent a great deal of time representing England in Europe and, being comptroller of the customs for wool and hides, he was a regular visitor to Southwark.

"His stature was not very tall:
Leane he was: his legs were small.
Hos'd within a stock of red:
A button bonnet on his head,
From under which did hang, I wene,
Silver haires both bright and sheene..."

Chaucer's *Canterbury Tales* became one of the best known narrative poems in the English language and established the reputation of Southwark hospitality worldwide. The Tabard itself has long since vanished from its site in Talbot Yard, off Borough High Street; only Tabard Street remains to remind visitors over 600 years later of Chaucer's timeless characters.

In Chaucer's day London Bridge offered the only carriageway across the Thames linking London and Southwark. The area developed from a need to provide accommodation, food and lively entertainment for the hundreds of bottlenecked merchants and travellers waiting their turn to enter the City. It became a meeting place for the best and the worst; a bubbling brew of music and drama, bawdy houses, flesh-mongers, theatres and several hundred inns. From the beginning the streets were noisy, overcrowded and often dangerous, mushrooming as they did in the swampy land along the river.

All this made Southwark the natural centre of London's entertainment industry – out of reach of the City's more stringent laws. Bankside attracted some of the most prodigious talents the English theatre has ever seen.

The best known of them all, William Shakespeare, has been claimed by his birthplace, Stratford-upon-Avon, as its own. The fact that Shakespeare's professional life as a playwright was rooted here, in 16th century Southwark, and that he wrote most of his plays for the Globe Theatre had been largely ignored until Sam Wanamaker's newly-built replica was opened.

Little is known about Shakespeare's personal life. As a contemporary of John Harvard, founder of America's first University, who lived in Borough High Street, he would have been a welcome part of the local social scene. His actor brother is buried in what is now Southwark Cathedral. Shakespeare appears to have led a somewhat less dissolute life than many of his colleagues. He became a shareholder of the new Globe Theatre and many of the settings and the characters he made famous were drawn from his knowledge and experience of Southwark.

That rumbustious old rogue, Sir John Falstaff, who bestrides Shakespeare's plays *Henry IV* and *Henry V*, was probably modelled on Southwark's Sir John Fastolf, who, in 1442, added to his already numerous and palatial homes by building a moated mansion on a site in Horsleydown. He willed money from his estates to various churches and chapels "for the wele of his sowle" so that prayers could be said for him for ever. This was not to be. On his death, in 1459 at the age of 82, a furore broke out over this will which was not settled for 13 years, by which time the prayers had been forgotten!

Thomas Doggett's claim to fame is not for his acting but as the founder of Britain's first annual sporting event. "Doggett's Coat and Badge" is a rowing race on the Thames, which preceded the Oxford and Cambridge Boat race by over 100 years. Early in the morning of 1 August 1721, the day of King George I's accession, a placard was posted on London Bridge: "This being the happy day of His Majesty's happy accession to the throne there will be given by Mr Doggett an orange coloured livery with a badge representing liberty to be rowed for by six watermen that are out of their time within the year past. They are to row from London Bridge to Chelsea. It will be continued annually on the same day for ever."

Close by London Bridge are the premises of The Worshipful Company of Glaziers – the only livery company on the south bank. But the greatest memorial to the Southwark School of Glaziers is not in the borough at all but in the glorious windows of Kings' College,

Cambridge. Between 1515-1531 Bernard Flower, Galyon Hone and Peter Nicholson, members of the School, produced some of the finest glass in Britain.

The development of literature too owes much to the skills of the printers of Southwark. In 1537, James Nicholson printed the first complete edition of The Bible and many other fine works were produced on the presses of St Thomas's Hospital.

Writers and artists have always gravitated to Southwark. Keats' House in St Thomas Street marks the former lodgings nearby of poet John Keats (1795-1821), who was a student at Guy's Hospital in 1815. There he was awarded the Certificate of Practical Medicine, which enabled him to practise as a doctor. It was here, too, that he wrote his early poems and *On First Looking into Chapman's Homer*. Turner's glorious vision of *The Fighting Temeraire* is a record of the ship's last journey towards Rotherhithe where she was to be broken up.

Some of the borough's most illustrious men and women are remembered in the names of streets and buildings. For instance, Brandon House, opposite St George's Church, Borough High Street, recalls Charles Brandon, Duke of Suffolk.

Borough High Street, 1830.

There, in 1545, when the house was owned by Henry VIII, a mint was established. The area then came to be notorious as "The Mint", a haunt of vagabonds and the destitute.

Mrs Elizabeth Newcomen was a philanthropist. In 1675 she left money to provide education and clothing for poor children. Her charity still helps young people today and Newcomen Street, off Borough High Street, keeps her memory alive.

Nearby, Ayres Street owes its name to the courage of a young children's nurse. On April 24 1885 Alice Ayres was caring for her three charges above an oil merchant's shop in Union Street. Fire broke out. But by the time Alice had rescued the children and thrown them from the window to the safe keeping of spectators below it was too late for Alice. Her hair and clothes were badly burned as she tried to jump and died later in hospital. Queen Victoria sent a personal message of condolence.

During the 19th century industrial explosion, dock development along the river, from Southwark to Greenwich, made the Port of London the "larder of the world". Factories were built and new industries moved into the area, bringing with them a new kind of personality – the owners, the bosses, the tycoons. They mostly lived in large houses in the countryside of Peckham, or Streatham, or even Brixton, but they made their mark in Southwark.

There was Mr Crosse and Mr Blackwell, Mr Peak and Mr Frean. In 1850 James Bowler made the first "hard hat", as an item of protective clothing for the future Earl of Leicester's gamekeepers. It was also used on building sites where top hats were frequently blown or knocked off. There were other 19th century individualists like Robert Barker who invented the Panorama. Mr Bryan Donkin was the first to produce tinned food in England and was delighted to receive a letter from the secretary to the Duke of Kent (Queen Victoria's father) "your patent beef was tasted by the Queen and Prince Regent and several distinguished personages and highly approved."

Puritanical Christian, Mr Robert Peacock Gloag, rolled the first British cigarettes in the Walworth Road in 1856. He had borrowed the idea from Russian soldiers he met during the Crimean War. In yellow paper with a hard cane tip, he sold it as "the cigarette you can bite on." There was uproar as moralists bemoaned the destruction of youth.

We have made our own journey in search of some of those pilgrims of the past; along the river Thames, from Blackfriars through Bankside to Bermonsey, on to Rotherhithe, and out towards Dulwich, returning through Camberwell and Walworth to The Borough itself. Along the way we have found so many memories of those men and women from Southwark, whose colourful and sometimes notorious lives have enriched British history. We have chosen a few of our favourites – there are so many, many more. This is their tale.

ALONG THE RIVER:
BANKSIDE, BERMONDSEY AND ROTHERHITHE

*Top: The Southwark section of the Braun and Hogenberg map of London, c.1560.
Right: A Thameside scene at Rotherhithe, 1914-15.*

JOHN OVERS

7TH CENTURY

ONCE UPON A TIME – so the legend goes – the only reliable way of reaching the City of London from Southwark was controlled by one man: John Overs. He monopolised the ferry business, owning a number of boats which carried passengers, horsemen, cattle and goods backwards and forwards across the Thames.

The Thames had made Overs rich but he was a miser and although his estate ranked with that of the wealthiest men in London he lived there in apparent poverty. His daughter Mary was, according to an 18th century tract *The True History of the Life and Sudden Death of Old John Overs*, "of a most beautiful aspect and a pious disposition who he had cared well to see liberally educated, though at the cheapest rate..."

So mean was he that he faked his own death in order to save a day's food and drink for his household. According to custom, servants were not permitted to take sustenance of any kind on the day their master died. He lay, his face whitened, beneath a sheet and surrounded by candles. But the plan failed. The servants celebrated and sang merrily as they ransacked the pantries and wine cellar.

When John Overs realised, from beneath the sheet, that all was not going well, he sat up – only to be hit on the head with a hammer by a menial who thought it was the devil rising in his master's body. This time John Overs was truly dead.

Meanwhile Mary Overs' lover set out for London by horse. He had heard of his future father-in-law's end and was anxious to ensure a stake in any inheritance. But his horse stumbled, he was fatally thrown and never saw Mary again.

Overs was buried in the Abbey of Bermondsey – but was promptly exhumed because the Abbot, who had been away at the time of the burial, knew he had been excommunicated. He had Overs' body tied to the back of a donkey and turned out with a prayer to God to direct the animal to a place suitable for a man of such bad character. The donkey off-loaded his burden at a place where a gibbet had once stood and it was there that John Overs was buried.

Mary had been left a very rich woman, plagued by suitors. She longed to escape from the world and the tragedies that had haunted her life. With the fortune left by her father she founded a House of Retreat. Around the year 852 AD, St Swithun, then Bishop of Winchester, turned the convent into a college for priests. The legend concludes that it was these priests, using the money bequeathed to the church by Mary Overs, who may have helped to build the very first, post-Roman, timber bridge across the Thames.

In fact the priory church of St Mary dates from the 12th century, and much later, became the parish church of St Saviour. Today, known as Southwark Cathedral, it is one of the oldest buildings in London.

KING OLAF of NORWAY

DIED 1030

GOLD IS WON and bright renown
London Bridge is broken down
Shields resounding
War horns sounding
Hildur shouting in the din!
Arrows singing
Mailcoats ringing
Odin makes our Olaf win!

This was the original version of the nursery rhyme written to celebrate the taking of London Bridge by Olaf the Norseman in 1014 at the Battle of Southwark.

Olaf, son of Odin, having been converted to Christianity, had become an ally of the Unready King Ethelred, who fled to France when the Danes took possession of most of England. In those days, the settlement of *Sudwerca* (Southwark) had been fortified and a bridge built to the City, wide enough to accommodate a two-way stream of traffic. Along the bridge were barricades which sheltered those defending it.

King Ethelred summoned a council at which Olaf suggested that if the King's army would work simultaneously with his ships, together they could oust the enemy.

Above: St Olaf as he appears on the exterior of St Olaf House, Tooley Street.

They began by pulling down a number of old houses and used the resulting materials to erect scaffolding over and down the sides of the ships. In this way Olaf estimated that his men should be able to attack under cover. The scaffolding was to be of such strength that it would withstand any onslaught from above. The plan didn't work. Once within sight of London Bridge the invasion force met with such a battering that helmets and swords were sent flying, ships were damaged and many of the men swam away.

So Olaf returned with his remaining forces, and on the ebb tide ingeniously managed to attach their craft by chains to the piles upon which the bridge was built. Helped by the current, they rowed hard until the piles gave way and the bridge collapsed, taking with it hundreds of defending soldiers. Many people were drowned and Southwark and the City were stormed and taken for Ethelred.

Amidst the rejoicings the first ever bardic songs were sung about London Bridge – from which the original version of the nursery rhyme itself was later drawn.

> "And thou has overthrown their Bridges, Oh thou Storm of the Sons of Odin! skillful and foremost in the Battle. For thee was it happily reserved to possess the land of London's winding City. Many were the shields which were grasped sword in hand to the mighty increase of the conflict: but by thee were the iron-banded coats of mail broken and destroyed."

After the battle, Olaf returned to his pious and Christian activities, and many churches including the now demolished St Olave in Tooley Street (itself a corruption of his name) were dedicated to his memory. His miraculous acts and beneficent works are recorded in many early manuscripts

Lightermen on the River Thames, c.1780

"Mark but THE WATERMAN attending to his fare,
Of hot and cold, of wet and dry, he always takes his share,
He carries bonny lasses over to the plays,
And here and there he gets a bit,
And that his stomach stays…"

JOHN TAYLOR (THE WATER POET)

1578-1653

John Taylor was the 17th century John Betjeman. He ran a thriving business, based in Southwark, carrying passengers to and fro in his wherries and recording every manoeuvre and almost every thought of his eventful, abundant career, in a prolific outpouring of lively comment and verse. Thames watermen were notorious for language spiced with oaths, abuse and topical ribaldry. By John Taylor's day this had become a tradition and he used it to defend his livelihood.

Born in Gloucester in 1578, John Taylor failed his Latin at school and was sent to be apprenticed as a Thames waterman. But before his seven year time was finished, like so many watermen, he was pressed into the Navy. During this period he made some sixteen voyages and was present at the Siege of Cadiz in 1596.

His sea adventures gave him a taste for travel which stayed with him all his life. He was one of the first to write travel guides for ordinary working people about Britain and Europe. His diaries were the equivalent of our own 20th century *Rough Guides* but they were not always reliable and there were those who doubted the truth of his stories! *The Pennyless Pilgrimage* was a frank, very personal, often amusing view of his last journey on foot "my legs I made my oars", from Southwark to Scotland "not carrying any Money to or fro, neither begging, borrowing, or asking meet, drink or lodging."

The Thames and Southwark were his first love and he ran his business in Southwark at a time when Bankside was noisily overbrimming with every conceivable form of entertainment that had been banned from the City. Shakespeare, Ben Jonson – John Taylor ferried the rich, the poor, the famous and infamous back and forth. Everyone knew him. He arranged pageants and composed triumphs for the Lord Mayors of London. No wonder he was anxious to protect his trade and became a militant defender of the watermen's cause against the rapidly increasing threat both from bridge building and traffic such as "upstart hell-cart-coaches". Some years before, in 1588, Queen Elizabeth herself had set the fashion by attending a thanksgiving service after the Spanish Armada in a "chariot throne" and the artistocracy and fashionable folk began to follow her example.

John Taylor wrote: " The first coach was a strange monster, it amazed both horse and man. Some said it was a great crab shell brought out of China: some thought it was one of the pagan temples, in which cannibals adored the devil. A coach or caroche" he railed " are mere engines of pride... a coach may fitly be compared to a whore, for a coach is painted, so is a whore, a coach is common, so is a whore, a coach is drawn with beasts, a whore is drawn away with beastly knaves. A coach hath loose curtains, a whore hath a loose gown, a coach is laced and fringed, so is a whore..."

He complained to Parliament that some 500 fares were being robbed from the watermen daily. Although he had limited success, so that for 35 years carriages were banned from approaching nearer than two miles to the river, his was a crusade against hopeless odds. In 1601 an Act to restrict the numbers of carts and carriages was rejected. Worse still, in 1603, an Act was passed which forbade anyone under the age of 18 years to carry passengers on the wherries "because it hath often happened that... divers and sundry people... have perished... through the unskilfulness... of the wherrymen..."

Undeterred, John Taylor, as usual, set pen to paper – his much publicised pamphlet *The World Runs on Wheels* was written to draw attention to his cause.

Yet another threat to the watermen arose after the death of Queen Elizabeth in 1603, when the theatres moved away from Southwark to the north side of the river. John Taylor once again spoke out for the beleaguered watermen. His pamphlet *The Cause of the Watermen's Suit Concerning Players* was an eloquent plea on behalf of the watermen who had so often fought at sea for King and Country.

In 1613 he presented a petition to King James I to prevent the building of a playhouse within four miles of the City on the north bank of the river. The players fought back and there was gossip that John Taylor had met them at the Cardinal's Hat on Bankside and accepted a bribe to let the suit fall. This was all too much for him and John Taylor set off again on a *"Verry-Merry-Wherry-Ferry-Voyage"* by sea to York.

On his return he discovered that one William Fennor had according to Taylor "arrogantly and falsely" claimed himself to be "the King's Majesty's rhyming Poet". True to form, Taylor challenged his rival to a trial of wit on the stage of the Hope Theatre, Bankside. He gave him 10 shillings to ensure his appearance and printed 1,000 bills inviting friends and neighbours to this "Bear Garden Banquet of dainty conceits." All seats were sold. But William Fennor, described by Taylor as "the rhyming rascal", never appeared. Needless to say Taylor wrote a vituperative tract, "because the ill-looking hound doth not confess he hath injured me, nor hath so much honesty as to bring or send me my money that he took in earnest off me..."

Towards the end of his life John Taylor retired from the river and became a very popular landlord of The Crown, an ale house in Long Acre on the north bank. Forever controversial, on the execution of King Charles I (1649) he changed the inn's name to The Mourning Bush as a declaration of his Royalist sympathies. But this caused such a rumpus that he changed the name yet again to The Poet's Head. He died in 1653.

Madame BRITANNICA HOLLANDIA

circa 1570-1633

There has been NO MORE COLOURFUL – if doubtful – contribution to the history of 16th and 17th century Southwark than that of *Madame* BRITANNICA HOLLANDIA and her HOUSE OF OBSENITIE. Situated in Paris Garden, it was said to be the most chic, most luxurious, best run whorehouse in Britain, attracting a very high-class clientele.

Opposite page: Holland's Leaguer, previously Paris Garden Manor House; Southwark's most exclusive brothel. A reprint of a 17th century view.

Mystery surrounds "Madame Hollandia". Her story is told in a tract, published in 1632, and was celebrated in prose, poems and plays. She is recorded, briefly, by William Shakespeare.

The story goes that as a little girl, brought up and educated in comfort (probably in Norfolk), she developed a precocious taste and talent for the life of the courtesan. Her unsuspecting parents sent her to London to stay with a wealthy, upperclass family to learn social graces. Instead, she met and married the prosperous Mr Holland, whose business interests in the City introduced her to a sparkling variety of gentlemen, who were captivated by her lustful, adolescent beauty. By the time she was 20 Elizabeth Holland had decided to become a Madame. In those days there were rules to regulate prostitution, and church, commercial and royal properties were all used as brothels. By reputation the brothel Madames were Flemish or French – hence Elizabeth's adopted fancy name.

She established a hugely successful business in the City, which was brought abruptly to an end by her imprisonment. The City's laws against Bawdy Houses had defeated her.

But across the river, in Southwark, no such laws existed. Somewhere between 1599 and 1602, after she had "talked" her way out of gaol, the lease of Paris Garden Manor House was granted to Elizabeth Holland. It was described in a later conveyance as "a Mansion House, within a mote, a gate house and four pastures ditched about." It was certainly a fine building, surrounded by a network of ditches, bridges and formal gardens. Nearby were all the excitements of the play houses and the dozens of ale houses and brothels. The area was rough and decidedly seedy and there was nothing to compete with the style envisaged by Southwark's newest resident.

"Holland's Leaguer", as it later became known, was restored to a state of grandeur, enabling it to attract the wealthiest clients in the land. Private rooms with comfortable beds were offered and, probably for the first time, the stench of close-stools on the landings was avoided by the introduction of a sweet-smelling "convenience", kept odour-free because it was sluiced into the Thames. The kitchens provided excellent food and wine to satisfy the clients' other appetites.

The girls were all fully trained in the art of sexual pleasure by Elizabeth herself. Her original team included: Beta Brestonia, an outstanding beauty and "impudent above all measure"; the tiny red-head Eliza Caunce; the well-educated, musical and ladylike Longa Maria (nothing was more irksome to her than "sleepe and silence"); and Maria Pettit "a smal handful of a woman".

Elizabeth Holland ran the place with the ferocity of a military campaigner. She made many enemies with her sharp tongue and authoritarian ways. Pikemen guarded the gates. A doctor was always on hand.

Through the 20 years of riotous success there is no record of Mr Holland, his role, or his reactions! He appears, only briefly, at the end of the story.

By 1625, when King Charles I came to the throne, Elizabeth was about 55 and her energies were flagging. Paris Garden had been self-governing and beyond the reach of the law. But one of King Charles's first ordinances was "Against Bawdy Houses". The rather straight-laced Charles cast something of a dampener on the world of the "luxurious impudent". His courtiers found it less easy to frequent their favourite amusements and this, together with a drift of the theatrical fraternity to new theatres across the water, meant business was less brisk.

In 1631 the authorities raided her "castle". Madame Hollandia was prepared: she had the portcullis pulled up and lured them on to the bridge. The bridge was then collapsed so that the intruders were thrown into stinking waters, whilst her ladies showered offal on them.

On January 26 1632 the Court of Star Chamber decreed: "Elizabeth, a woman of ill repute, and her husband were called uppon an intimation of £100 but they did not appear. Therefore another intimation of £200." The following year, in February, the Star Chamber recorded that Elizabeth had gone away. That was the last history knows of her. She vanished, the house was sold and she disappeared from the records.

As the ballad said:
"Holland's Leaguer is lately upbroken
This for a certaine is spoken".

JOHN RENNIE 1761-1821
and SIR JOHN RENNIE 1794-1874

NORTH WEST of the site of PARIS GARDEN Manor House, running south from the river between Kings Reach and Stamford Street, is Rennie Street, which commemorates one of the world's greatest engineering giants, John Rennie, the last of the great stone bridge builders.

Born in Scotland, Rennie arrived in London in 1784. He was just 23 and was employed to help with the building of the revolutionary Albion Mill, alongside Blackfriars Bridge. The six-storey mill had no external quays, and boats sailed into a basement lagoon for loading and unloading. It was Rennie's job to design milling machinery to be powered by two of the largest of James Watt's new steam engines, which had been installed.

One hundred years later results were described by engineers as "one of the best pieces of that class of engineering ever constructed, either before or since". The marvel was Rennie's first use of metal for driving shafts and gears – a model for future engineers. Even the great Brunel followed where Rennie had led.

In the spring of 1791, the mills were destroyed by fire and never restored. Rennie bought the land and a row of deserted houses in Holland Street (now Hopton Street) and set up a thriving engineering machinery business. Here, it is claimed, in the 18th century, was the home of Nell Gwynn, the mistress of King Charles II.

In 1789, John Rennie married 19 year old Martha MacKintosh, at Christ Church, Blackfriars Road. She was a homely woman, dedicated

*John Rennie, senior
Southwark's engineering genius.*

to her role as a wife and mother. They moved to Stamford Street in "one of the most fashionable suburbs of the metropolis". There she bore nine children, of whom six survived. George, the eldest, was born in 1791 and John junior in 1794. It seems to have been an unruly family, with father remote and preoccupied.

When Martha died in 1806, John Rennie's sister Henrietta took over running the household but the Southwark air was too dank for her and eventually she returned to Scotland. George wrote to her in 1815 "... we have felt your loss extremely... the children... have been running wild for want of a person capable of controlling them; for although their father has great command when he pleases yet he sees them so seldom that his authority cannot often be enough applied... Conceive the children left to themselves in the Parlour, the room in a perfect mess of rubbish and confusion, things lying here and there..."

At that time the family was living in some style; they had a governess, six servants and a coachman to look after the new "chariot" with its smart harness and two horses.

John Rennie was far too deeply immersed in his Southwark engineering works to seek the acclaim he justly deserved. He was appointed chief engineer in charge of the building of Waterloo, Southwark and London Bridges; he solved the problems of the East India and London Docks; supervised the construction of the Kennet and Avon Canal, Newhaven Harbour, and Plymouth Docks – and a seemingly limitless number of major projects abroad.

Later, in 1817, he even refused a knighthood for his work on the building of three of London's great bridges. Uncommercial and publicity-shy, his brilliant and original mind placed him far ahead of his engineering and inventing peers. But he never bothered to patent his ideas and others often reaped the glory.

He built macadamised roads long before McAdam. His revolutionary plans for dock restraining walls were eventually patented by Samuel Bentham. He perfected the use of ball bearings around 1791, but Robert Stevenson was given the credit for this in 1810. Even James Watt was jealous and afraid of him and begged Rennie not to compete with him in the development of the steam engine. For Rennie the development of such ideas was simply part of the day's work and he was open and happy to share them with anyone.

In 1821, Rennie senior was commissioned to produce designs for the new London Bridge, a task he started but never completed. He had always been a workaholic who "rarely took play". He rose at five every morning and never retired until midnight. This daily routine took its toll and in the late summer of that year he died, with his sons and daughters by his side. He was buried in St Paul's Cathedral.

In a biography of his father, in almost unintelligible handwriting many years later, his son John, wrote: "his personal appearance was very dignified and imposing. He was nearly 6' 4" tall... and in his prime could and did walk 50 miles in a day without fatigue and could easily lift three cwts upon his little finger. His head was extremely fine and majestic with a broad oval countenance, large expressive blue eyes... and splendid luxurious auburn hair..."

George, Rennie's eldest son, was brilliant but lame and second son John had already been taken into the business. Although the brothers did not always see eye to eye – George was a strict Presbyterian and disapproved of John's flamboyant style – on their father's death, George decided to join the family business and their partnership was a great success. The Rennie enterprises had become internationally renowned. Eventually they decided to build much larger workshops in Woolwich and in the 1870's their Southwark premises were pulled down to make way for the railway.

But it was John Rennie senior's legacy, the building of London Bridge, which was to make his son's name and bring him the knighthood which his more retiring father had rejected. John's aunt wrote at the time: "Whereas his father was interested in the building of memorable constructions, John it would seem is more interested in proffering the shoulder for accolades." Accolades there certainly were, when, in 1831 the new London Bridge was finally opened. It had cost two and a half million pounds and forty lives.

King William IV commanded that there should be a procession by water and a magnificent pavilion with a throne was erected over the northern end of the bridge. The river was spectacular with gilded barges, streamers and hundreds of boats carrying the sightseeing public.

In 1874 Sir John Rennie died. All that remains in Southwark to mark the borough's links with this great family is the narrow street named after them.

In 1968, Rennie's London Bridge was sold for £1 million. 10,000 tons of the original 130,000 tons of stone were shipped over the Atlantic and across the United States to the Arizona desert, where it was reconstructed in the new city of Havasu.

Flamboyant son, Sir John Rennie.

SAM WANAMAKER

1919-1993

For many years, the "UPSTART" AMERICAN ACTOR Sam Wanamaker was an irritating thorn in the side of Southwark Council.

Sam had been born to extreme poverty in a Jewish ghetto in Chicago and had 'escaped" in 1949 from General McCarthy's Communist witch-hunt. He made a sensational British stage debut in 1952, in Clifford Odett's *Winter Journey*, and went on to become the London theatre's favourite star.

Exploring the streets of Bankside and Borough as a young man, he was shocked to find that not only was there no commemoration of William Shakespeare's original theatre, The Globe, but that, worse, there was virtually no recognition of Southwark's most famous son. So, at the peak of his theatrical career, Sam Wanamaker decided to change course and to devote the rest of his life to correcting this wrong.

He bought a house in Falmouth Road, Southwark and began to bully, harry and hassle not only the local authority but individuals and companies worldwide. He was obsessed.

He needed over £20 million to erect his replica of Shakespeare's Globe. 20 sided, three storeys high, it was made of timber, wattle and daub and open to the air. It was to be a people's theatre, as it had been in the 16th century. He wanted the building to be at the heart of an international cultural centre with a museum, study facilities and a hotel. No one believed he could succeed but it was his "Holy Grail".

Originally the Council was supportive and agreed a deal with a property company which would finance a riverside site at Greenmore Wharf, in return for planning permission to build an office block. The Council was promised some half a million visitors a year to The Globe development, in addition to jobs and prestige. As part of the deal they agreed to relocate twelve roadsweepers who operated from the proposed site. Michael Heseltine, then Secretary of State for the Environment, gave the go-ahead and Sam seemed home and dry.

But then there was an election and a new hard-line Labour council reneged on the agreement.

They fought Sam tooth and nail. They wanted to put a housing development on the proposed site. They first accused him of elitism and egotism and then of wanting to create a Disneyland-on-Thames. They claimed it was all a tourist gimmick. They even objected, in desperation, that the twelve roadsweepers at Greenmore Wharf had nowhere else to store their equipment!

Eventually, Sam won a High Court battle which cost Southwark Council over £9 million and, in 1986, he was granted a 125 year lease. Work began. It was to be, as Sam himself said "an epic journey through an ocean of icebergs."

There were warm patches too. The Duke of Edinburgh agreed to be patron. The late Sir John Gielgud, Dame Judi Dench, Sir Anthony Hopkins, Diana Rigg and Derek Jacobi were all amongst the original Globe Theatre Trust directors. The names of Getty, Rothschild, Hammer and Fairbanks were already on the list of donors.

The project was defiantly ambitious and complex. Before any work could begin it was necessary to build a 40ft diaphragm wall to protect the building from the river. Also, for example, the Norfolk thatch had to be soaked in fire retardant and laid over fireproof boarding fitted with a hidden sprinkler system.

In 1989 first the remains of the original Rose Theatre and then the Globe were discovered nearby. Doubters suddenly saw what Sam had seen years before – that Bankside was the Broadway of its day. But Sam called a halt to further work on the project; his declared reason was that they should wait to see the physical structure of the original building instead of relying on documentary evidence. The truth was that money had run out.

Sam, wearing his now familiar yellow hard hat, assumed a Churchillian strength and determination. He knew, what no one else knew, that he had prostate cancer and time for him was dangerously short. He did not tell his family.

His energy was phenomenal. There is no doubt that he often exhausted his team, but without his visionary drive and genial powers of persuasion and publicity flair there would have been no Globe today.

Hours after the remains of The Globe were uncovered Sam's latest publicity sensation arrived from America. It was a 30ft by 20ft banner, which had taken a young designer Gordon Schwontkowski 700 hours to paint. It bore the brave legend, from *Hamlet*, "This Grave Shall have a Living Monument"; it was a sentiment endorsed by Sam and doubted by almost everyone else.

The vast muddy site lay idle through 1990-91 and a threatened recession. Fund raising was almost impossible; it was described as "London's largest swimming pool". The deadlock was broken by the vision, not this time of Sam, but of his architect, Theo Crosby. He proposed a self-build scheme in which they would "do it themselves" using out-of-work local builders and craftsmen and so creating a friendly, involved team, much as would have built the original theatre.

Sam's legacy: the reconstruction of the Globe Theatre on Bankside.

It worked. On Shakespeare's birthday, April 23rd, in 1993 Sir John Gielgud spoke the dedication words within "this wooden O". The event was attended by many stage stars and by Princess Michael of Kent. The inaugural production was typically idiosyncratic – it was in German! Of course most of the finance for the theatre had come from abroad.

It was a tragedy of Shakespearian proportions that, when Sam Wanamaker's Globe Theatre was finally opened to the public in 1994 in the presence of The Queen and Prince Philip, neither Sam nor his devoted wife, Charlotte, were there to hear the applause. He had died of cancer, broken hearted, on 16 December 1993. Charlotte died soon after. Theo Crosby too had died on 12 September 1994.

Today, the theatre is, as he dreamed it would be all those years ago, the focus of a cultural complex. 250,000 enthusiasts visit the theatre annually and 300,000 tour the exhibition.

MRS THRALE 1741-1821
and DR SAMUEL JOHNSON 1709-1784

FOUR FOOT ELEVEN INCHES TALL, the tiny chestnut-haired Mrs Hester Thrale became the leading literary hostess of her day. She was charming, witty, effusive and impulsive: it was said by a friend "she is the first woman in the world could she but restrain that wicked tongue of hers. She would be the only woman in the world could she but command that little whirligig."

In 1763, at the age of 22, Hester had come to live in Southwark as the young bride of old Etonian, Henry Thrale, whom she had married only to please her mother. She did not love him. He had inherited Child's Brewery (later Barclay Perkins) on Bankside from his father, a house in Deadman's Place near the brewery and a country mansion in Streatham. Commuting from Streatham to the brewery was extremely dangerous and since her husband was so often set upon by footpads and vagabonds they were forced to spend the weekdays in Southwark, which she hated. In 1764 her first child, Queenie, was born, to be followed, over the next fourteen years, by one boy and nine girls, only four of whom survived. Hester Thrale blamed the disagreeable air and conditions in Southwark for their deaths.

Bored with domesticity Hester began writing and it was on Bankside in 1765 that she first met her husband's friend, Dr Samuel Johnson, already famous for his Dictionary. Their friendship lasted for nearly 20 years.

Johnson, who was physically repulsive, frightened her at first, but he became relaxed and flirtatious in her company, although the friendship remained platonic. He was given a room of his own, both at Streatham and in Southwark. He could often be seen taking a walk in the garden opposite the house, his back stooped, his black stockings wrinkled and his faded coat badly worn. At Mrs Thrale's suggestion he was diverted from shuffling around the brewery itself because his absent mindedness and short sight made him a menace to the draymen and porters.

For Dr Johnson, the Thrales were his family. He busied himself with all their interests, especially the children. He helped Henry Thrale with his electioneering. Hester seemed to draw confidences from him and rare, warm, good humour, as night after night she stayed up, making tea and conversation, comforting his insomnia.

Although he was more than 30 years her senior, she was the light in the life of the learned, unhappy misfit. Plump, pretty, with a good complexion, her face adorned with the fashionable rouge and patches of the time, she was vivacious and well-informed. But she was no blue stocking – her friends called her a "rattle".

She told Boswell: "there are many who admire and respect Dr Johnson, but you and I love him".She treated Johnson with affection and respect,persuading him to change his scruffy, patched coat from time to time, to take medicine for his catarrh and always to change his candle-scorched wigbefore entering their dining room.

Lovesick Dr Johnson

It was largely thanks to Dr Johnson that Mrs Thrale met so many celebrated writers and artists and became herself a magnet to them. Over the next 20 years Oliver Goldsmith, Sir Joshua Reynolds, David

Garrick the actor, Edmund Burke, Fanny Burney and James Boswell all graced her table in Southwark.

Boswell recalls arriving at breakfast one day in 1776 to be welcomed by Johnson "in a full glow of conversation" and being given hot chocolate to sustain him. "I felt quite restored", he says.

Johnson successfully urged Hester herself to write and so she kept a record of these sparkling gatherings in a commonplace-book, exactly as they happened. She wrote as she talked, pouring her thoughts and her poetry on to paper in a torrent of often repetitive, unpunctuated words.

In the Spring of 1776, the Thrales' only son, nine year old Harry, died leaving Henry in a state of black despair, a very sick man. His health was not improved by worry over the Gordon Riots. In 1780, mobs, opposed to the easing of restrictions on Roman Catholics, surged around the narrow streets of London, yelling "no Popery" and burning everything they could lay their hands on. In Bankside their target was the brewery; they thought Henry Thrale was a Papist because he believed that Roman Catholics should be treated equally. The attack was brilliantly diverted by an astute manager, John Perkins, who entertained the mob at a nearby ale house and got them all drunk and incapable!

In 1781 Henry Thrale died, leaving his affairs in poor shape.

Many people hoped that Mrs Thrale would marry Johnson, who was by now 72. But instead she fell in love with the handsome but unsuitable Italian, Gabriel Piozzi, her children's music tutor and in 1782 she finally severed the link with her unhappy friend. She was full of remorse and near breakdown with divided loyalty. Dr Johnson was bitter, angry and heartbroken and burnt all her letters. "Almighty God, Father of all Mercy, help me by thy grace that I may, with humble and sincere thankfulness remember the comforts and conveniences which I have enjoyed at this place." In 1784 he too died.

By the time she died, in 1821, Mrs Thrale had penned over 1,000 pages of her commonplace-book – including a unique insight into their memorable friendship.

DR ALFRED SALTER

1873-1945

Dr Alfred Salter and his beloved wife Ada DEDICATED THEIR LIVES TO THE SERVICE OF BERMONDSEY and its poor – devotion which, ironically, rewarded them with tragedy and unhappiness.

For nearly fifty years the tall upright figure of Alfred Salter was a much loved and welcome sight. He cycled everywhere, because he did not want to set himself above his patients by driving a car. Even as a student he was nicknamed "Citizen Salter" for his pacifism, his radical socialism and crusading energy in pursuit of a better life for the poor.

Alfred Salter was born in 1873, in Greenwich, the son of an amateur vet and gas-board official. He was a boisterous boy with a passion for collecting tadpoles, beetles and other creepy-crawlies – to the despair of his house-proud mother. At the age of sixteen he won a scholarship to Guy's Hospital and so skeletons and medical specimens were added to his collection. His enthusiasm for life was formidable but his awareness of slum housing conditions and his own experience of tuberculosis as a student accelerated the development of his social conscience.
He graduated in 1895 and went on to carry out research at the Lister Institute where he learned his lifelong habit of wearing gloves at all times.

In 1897 he described how, in Bermondsey, there was often just "one stand pipe for 25 houses and the water supply on for only 2 hours a day. Never on Sundays. Before going to work people are forced to queue in the snow and rain for the one water closet serving all these houses. What is the use of my mending bodies when the social environment breaks them all the time?" he despaired.

In 1898 he took up residence in the Bermondsey Settlement. This was a purpose-built Gothic-style mansion which housed a very active community centre. Founded by Dr Scott Lidgett it provided educational and social activities of all kinds with some accommodation. When Dr Salter moved in he became a "jumping firework", brimming with ideas for ways of making life better for local people. There too, he fell in love with Ada Brown, in charge of the girls' club. She was five years his senior and in contrast a quiet, devoted Quaker. In 1900 they were married and soon after Dr Salter was offered the opportunity for professional promotion. He decided to reject the certainty of following in the footsteps of Pasteur or Lister and to stay, humbly, among his patients in Bermondsey.

"I have no lingering hankering" he wrote to Ada "after the flesh-pots of Guy's or Harley Street." She backed what she saw as his "divine vocation". She replied to his letter: "we are to be given over to the service of Bermondsey, to be her faithful servants and, if necessary, to give our lives for her".

Together they opened a surgery near Jamaica Road; it was a partnership that was to bring about a revolution in the area. In 1902 their daughter, Joyce, was born and in 1906 they moved to 5 Storks Road, a grimy three-storeyed building overhung by a large factory.

They shared a love of nature and the countryside and Ada soon transformed their yard into a "green parlour" hung with creepers and flowers; it was considered to be a local miracle. Gradually Dr Salter began to dream of a creating a garden city, with tree-lined streets and houses with bathrooms.

In 1908 he founded the first branch of the Labour Party in Bermondsey. He bought an ancient printing press and gathered a team of local workers to print leaflets night and day. He also paid for a column to plead the socialist cause in the local paper and so put Bermondsey on the political map for the first time. He was the first to raise funds through garden parties, with races and stalls and even started a children's playground.

Left: Alfred Salter with his beloved daughter Joyce.
Above: Ada Salter.

All this time the Salters' little girl, Joyce, was attending the local school. They had agreed not to send her away to a Quaker school – a supreme test of their ideals, because they felt they could not withdraw her from her friends on the street. She played with the rough, tough kids of the area, who were welcomed for tea at the Salter house, but when they left all Joyce's toys were disinfected. It was to no avail. Joyce caught scarlet fever three times and in 1910 she died at the age of eight. Months passed before her parents smiled again and every day flowers were placed by her photograph in the living room. Somehow this tragic sacrifice made Alfred and Ada identify even more with Bermondsey. It became a passion.

In November 1910 Ada was the first woman councillor in London and the only Independent Labour Party councillor elected to the local council.

During the First World War, when he was a vociferous pacifist, Alfred bought Fairby Grange, at Hartley in Kent, and turned it into a convalescent home for the people of Bermondsey and for conscientious objectors who had been broken by prison.

In the 1922 General Election Labour won Bermondsey for the first time, and Alfred Salter became its M.P. He cycled to the House of Commons and took groups of socialist colleagues on the 47 bus to Kent for weekend country walks.

That same year Ada was elected Mayor and formed a Beautification Committee to transform the outward appearance of the borough. Fairby was used as a nursery for trees and gradually the Salters began to realise their unlikely dream of the garden city. Flowers were planted everywhere "like vases in a dusty room". In two years over 9,000 were planted, window boxes and plants appeared in yards and outside public buildings and prizes were awarded for the best gardens. The *Daily Chronicle* spoke of "Bermondsey Boulevards".

The plan was breathtaking and unique but it was cosmetic. Dr Salter (whose medical practice in the meantime was growing by leaps and bounds) urged the demolition of two thirds of the houses in

Bermondsey, which he said were unfit to live in. He wanted the population rehoused in modern homes designed as garden suburbs or moved out to the fringes of London and a better transport service provided. Many Bermondsey people were in fact re-housed on the Downham Estate in Lewisham and Bromley.

In 1926 he opened a solarium which was the best equipped TB treatment centre in Britain and so cut deaths by half. Nearby, from 1927, was a "Palace of Baths", a magnificent place of marble and stained glass which would, according to the *Daily Mirror* "satisfy the most luxury loving Roman patrician". Alongside their concern for public health the Salters were also anxious to provide open spaces and play areas for children.

By 1928 people were coming from all over Europe to see what he was doing. But it was all stopped by the depression. That year he showed the first signs of exhaustion from his incredibly energetic lifestyle and 30 years continuous strain. He felt a failure in parliament and became depressed and was heartbroken by the realisation that his large-scale garden city dreams were far too expensive. The idea was abandoned.

In 1938 he was ill and fell into a coma but once again pulled round. The outbreak of War caused him utter despair – he had not believed it could happen. He developed thrombosis of the brain and lost his speech and tragically, at the same time, Ada too was ill and they went together to a nursing home.

His world seemed to be collapsing. He felt humiliated when the Labour party abandoned pacifism and became a grey, silent figure watching his Bermondsey flock suffer as the bombs destroyed their homes. When Ada died, in 1942, Alfred lost the will to live. He died in 1945, a recluse, with his beloved Bermondsey and all he had worked for apparently in ruins about him. Yet the memory of the man and his work remains and he is still greatly respected and his achievements spoken of with admiration.

SIR MARC BRUNEL 1769-1849
and ISAMBARD K. BRUNEL 1806-1859

Southwark owes its links with the GENIUS of MARC and ISAMBARD BRUNEL to the existence of the common ship worm – Teredo Navalis – which destroys timber.

Sir Marc Brunel (left) and his son Isambard Kingdom (right)

It was this worm which inspired French-born Marc Brunel in the design of the Thames Tunnel between Rotherhithe and Wapping. This was the world's first under-river tunnel for public traffic. He observed the movement of the worm's wood-crunching jaws and its method of self-propulsion, and designed a huge tunnelling shield honeycombed into 34 separate cells. Each cell was faced with oak planks. Inside it a man removed the planks in turn, hacked out the tunnel face and then, replacing each plank, jacked himself forward into a new position – much like the worm. Teams of masons and bricklayers lined the face behind the shield.

The royalist Brunel had arrived in England from America in 1799. He had escaped from republican France and then prospered as Chief Engineer of New York.

He married his English sweetheart, Sophia Kingdom, and they had three children. Marc was a loving, unassuming husband and father, a musician and an artist. In those early years in Britain he was granted 17 patents which were to prove vital to the development of industry and invented a set of machines that automated the production of pulleys for the Royal Navy.

But Brunel's enthusiasm as a respected engineer exceeded his bank balance and in 1816, two years after becoming a member of the Royal Society, he and Sophia found themselves languishing in a dank cell in the King's Bench Debtors' Prison, Southwark. Their debts were cleared by the Government, after intervention by the Duke of Wellington, who had recognised Brunel's genius.

By 1820 traffic through Southwark was almost at a standstill. Some 4,000 horse-drawn carts and wagons attempted to cross London Bridge daily and the same number of foot passengers were carried by the 350 ferryboats weaving between the huge cargo ships lying alongside the wharves. Access to the rapidly expanding "world's larder" of the docks was gridlocked. There was no bridge downriver of London Bridge. The answer to the paralysis which threatened trade and was strangling Southwark seemed to lie with the inspired young inventor and engineer, Marc Brunel.

In 1823 he proposed and exhibited his plans for a tunnel beneath the Thames with a shaft at either end. It was well received and encouraged especially by the Duke of Wellington.

The Brunels came to live in Southwark in 1824 because Marc needed to be near the site of the tunnel.

After a great deal of planning, publicity, fund raising and preliminary surveying, The Thames Tunnel Company was formed in 1824 with Brunel as Engineer to the Company. In 1825 work began on the shaft on the Rotherhithe side. At 1 o'clock on 2 March 1825 Marc Brunel laid the first brick and his diminutive son, Isambard, the second. A superb icing sugar model of the tunnel had been prepared especially for the occasion which was attended by a large number of respectable guests, including a Red Indian Chief, Little Carpenter! The construction of the tunnel cost 10 lives, £614,000 and was delayed by five floods.

Isambard Kingdom Brunel was already showing signs that he had inherited his father's talent. He was educated by his father till the age of nine and then sent to college in France. At the age of 16 he joined his father's office, working from the house in Southwark. So when Marc eventually collapsed from exhaustion and was unable to supervise the tunnelling, Isambard became resident engineer, at the age of 19, on a project that was being watched by the entire western world.

Like his father, Isambard was a hands-on engineer. He sometimes stayed underground for thirty-six hours at a time. From the outset work was bedevilled by problems. Men fell ill with river fever and several of his close colleagues died. In 1827, to Isambard's fury, the directors of The Thames Tunnel Company decided to raise funds by admitting spectators at one shilling a time. Despite his fear that the tunnel could collapse with horrific consequences, over 700 spectators were admitted daily. Sure enough on May 18th, just after Lady Raffles and a group of aristocrats had left the site, the water rose and a torrent flooded the tunnel. This time no lives were lost. Work was suspended.

Marc Brunel suffered a stroke but, despite his loss of speech and clumsy movements, he organised a banquet in the tunnel in November 1827 to celebrate the resumption of digging. The following year, on January 12th, an immense wave of water swept through the excavations propelling Isambard 42ft upwards – to safety – at the top of the Rotherhithe shaft. Women and children in their night clothes huddled at the entrance to hear the fate of their menfolk. Six died that night and Isambard, with no regard for his own safety and despite injuries, insisted on being taken down on a mattress in the diving bell to inspect the damage. Now half way across the river, the tunnel face was covered with a mirror and visitors brought down for one shilling a time.

The tunnel remained silent and empty for six years, until in 1835 Parliament voted more money for its completion.

From then the main problem facing the tunnellers was fire damp (natural gas) but eventually, on a proud day in 1841, 15 years after his project was launched, Marc Brunel, now aged 72, his son Isambard and toddler grandson walked in triumph through the completed passage under the river. Marc was knighted, and the tunnel formally opened by Queen Victoria in January 1843. In July that year Queen Victoria, Prince Albert and a small entourage, accompanied by the Tunnel Company directors, enjoyed an impromptu walk from Wapping to Rotherhithe and back. *The Times* reported: "The very walls were in a cold sweat."

Thames watermen flew black flags in protest, fearing loss of passenger trade. They need not have feared, for the tunnel quickly lost its appeal. Only accessible still by the two 80ft shafts, there was no more money to build ramps which would take carriages through the tunnel and so relieve congestion above. This magnificent construction became the haunt of whores and thieves. It was a design triumph, an inspiration for others to follow. But it was also a complete financial flop. Southwark's traffic congestion was far from over.

In 1865 the tunnel was sold to the East London Railway Company and today carries the East London Line between New Cross and Whitechapel.

PRINCE LEE BOO

1764-1784

ON A SUMMER DAY, 14 July 1784, a carriage bringing a bewildered very special passenger drew into Rotherhithe after eight months at sea and a 12 hour journey from Portsmouth. The young man was Prince Lee Boo -19 year old son of the King of Pelau, a group of remote islands in the South Pacific. He spoke almost no English yet his charm and good nature were to win the hearts of everyone he met. He had arrived in England with little more than a length of rope in which he tied knots to mark each stage of his great adventure.

Lee Boo was welcomed and cared for by Captain Henry Wilson and his family at 28 Paradise Row, Rotherhithe, where his arrival was marked by another knot in the rope.

On August 10th the year before, Captain Wilson of the East India Company's ship *The Antelope* was shipwrecked between the Philippines and the Carolinas. The Captain and his crew were cared for in style for over two months by King Abba Thule, who encouraged them to build a new boat. *The Oroolong* was completed by November and when their guests were ready to sail The King asked Wilson to take his son Lee Boo to England "to make him an Englishman".

According to the Captain's friend George Keate, who wrote a book about Lee Boo, Wilson agreed that he would "endeavour to merit the high trust reposed in him by treating the young Prince with the same tenderness and affection as his own son". Lee Boo and young Harry Wilson soon became great friends playing together. The Prince called Henry Wilson's wife, Christiana, "mother" and couldn't bear to hear of any friction.

Keate recalls how, once after Harry had been reprimanded, "Lee Boo took his young friend by the hand and on entering into the parlour went up to the father, and laying hold of his hand joined it with that of his son, and pressing them together, dropped over both those tears of sensibility, which his affectionate heart could not occasion suppress".

Keate described his first meeting with the boy. "He was dressed as an Englishman, excepting that he wore his hair in the fashion of his country;... was of middling stature, and had a countenance so strongly marked with endearing good-humour and sensibility that it constantly prejudiced everyone in his favour; and this countenance was enlivened by eyes so quick and intelligent, that they might really be said to announce his thoughts and conceptions without the aid of language."

Life in Rotherhithe was full of excitement: long walks along the river to watch the sailmakers, ropemakers, carters and porters, the famous Greenland Dock where tall-masted whalers floated on an inland pool and strolls around the farms and gardens, past windmills and orchards. He was taken to St Mary's Church where, according to Keate, "he could not comprehend the service but perfectly understood the intent". He also watched the first ever balloon flight above English soil, by an

Italian, Lunardi, who took off to the astonishment of thousands of spectators and the Prince of Wales.

When Captain Wilson was summoned to East India House to explain the loss of *The Antelope*, Lee Boo went along too – wearing a pink coat with a green collar and brown lapels, a striped waistcoat and black necktie. They walked over London Bridge and into the City of London.

Every day Lee Boo went to school. Within a few months he had picked up a remarkable command of English and was even giving autographs to pupils and teachers with whom he was equally popular. He seems to have had the knack of making everyone he met feel better.

The time was approaching when Captain Wilson felt that Lee Boo's stay in England had been well spent and that he should return home to Pelau. But it was not to be. There was one more knot to be tied in his rope.

On 18 December 1784 Lee Boo felt unwell. He had smallpox. He was alone, because none of the family was allowed to see him, but even then his concern seems to have been for them. He took the surgeon by the hand, and, "fixing his eyes steadfastly on him, with earnestness said: 'good friend, when you go to Pelew tell Abba Thulle take much drink to make the small pox go away but he die... that the Captain and Mother... very kind... all English very good men... was much sorry that he could not speak to the King the number of fine things the English had got'".

He died on December 27. The Reverend Edward Beck said of his interment: "He was interred in Rotherhithe Churchyard, the Captain and his brother attending. The young people of the academy were present and a great concourse of parishioners thronged the church."

SOUTH TO PECKHAM, DULWICH AND CAMBERWELL

Peckham Rye, 1810, a watercolour by John Brompton Cuming.

DR HAROLD ARUNDEL MOODY

1882-1947

TO BE HIS PATIENT, they said, WAS TO BE HIS FRIEND. Dr Harold Moody, the black physician who cared for the people of Peckham for over 30 years, has been compared to Dr Martin Luther King. A huge man in every way, kindly Dr Moody was known as the children's doctor – they loved him for his gentle manner and hearty laugh.

Harold Moody defied prejudice and broke new ground throughout his life. He was a born fighter but whatever hostility might have existed on account of his colour was overwhelmed through "his charm, his devotion and his skill."

He came to England from Jamaica in 1904. He trained at King's College and the Royal Eye Hospital at St George's Hospital, where he met a young white nurse Mabel Tranter. Against every taboo they fell in love. When he qualified in 1912 he found that a black doctor was not welcome in most London hospitals, but eventually he was offered work at the Marylebone Medical Mission where he combined the post of doctor and conductor of religious services.

The Cycling Parson of Wimbledon, the Reverend Fred Hastings, helped him by inviting the devout doctor to preach one Sunday at his Peckham church. He got on well with the local people and it was here that he decided to put down roots. With money advanced, most unusually, by the bank he bought 111 Kings Road as his family home and surgery and here the elegant doctor in his dark suit and tie gradually won the complete confidence of the local residents.

Mabel Tranter and Harold Moody were married at Holy Trinity Church, Henley-on-Thames in May 1913, despite the earnest protestations of both their families. However Mabel's mother was courageous enough to ignore convention and was present at the ceremony. The cake was baked by his mother in Jamaica and iced in London.

Theirs was a spectacularly successful marriage, resulting in six high-achieving children. Christine became a pioneer doctor in the early days of the World Health Organisation, son Harold, also a doctor, won gold medals at the 1950 Empire Games; they both served in the forces in India during World War II. Arundel and Garth were the first black commissioned officers in the British army.

In July 1919 Dr Moody decided to return, for a holiday, to Jamaica, with his family, leaving his patients in the care of his newly qualified brother, Ludlow.

The odyssey was a sad disappointment. In America Dr Moody found himself prevented from sharing a beach with whites and he was distressed by the poor schooling, illegitimacy and social conditions in his homeland. He returned to London determined to crusade in the name of God, his Christian faith and his race. "I pray to God to give me grace, strength, ability and tact to do something to show the world that character and not colour is the thing of ultimate importance. I will not, and shall not, apologise for my birth."

In 1922 the family moved to 164 Queens Road, Peckham and Dr Moody joined the Camberwell Green Congregational Church. He was the first black man to be appointed chairman of the Board of Directors of the Colonial Missionary Society and later, in 1931, he became first President of the newly-formed League of Coloured Peoples and champion of black people in Britain. Continually he was called on to represent black nurses who were refused work in British hospitals. When the internationally famous West Indian cricketer, Learie Constantine, was refused accommodation in a London hotel, Dr Moody led the protests.

With Mrs Moody supporting him, he was able to undertake a ferocious timetable of public engagements. In one year alone he addressed 264 meetings at 84 centres, travelling 364 air miles, 5974 train miles and 10184 road miles still leaving time for his cricket and his stamp collection. This was a pattern that continued throughout his career.

In 1944 a rocket exploded at New Cross, among the Christmas shopping crowds of mainly mothers and children, causing the country's heaviest casualties of the war. 200 people died and many hundreds were injured. Dr Moody was there as part of the team called in from all surrounding areas, struggling night and day amidst the carnage to bring comfort. There were cars in flames, collapsed buildings and scores of dazed blood-drenched victims, many in agonising pain.

There was to be a tragic twist in the tail of his life. In 1946 Dr and Mrs Moody left England for a five month journey to America and the West Indies. Their mission was to present the case for the economic and

social betterment of the West Indies and the establishment of a £250,000 cultural centre for coloured people in London. Dr Moody talked with politicians, trade unions, church officials and social workers all over the Caribbean and the journey was officially recognised.
He was honoured by a banquet given by the Governor, Sir John, and Lady Huggins in Government House. On a personal level it was made all the more special by a Christmas Day family reunion, presided over by his mother.

On the way back to England, he drafted a lengthy report for Arthur Creech Jones, Parliamentary Secretary for the West Indies, but by the time he was back in Peckham he was ill. Despite a high fever he worked on this report with his church minister the Rev. David Vaughan, but on 24 April 1947 he died, at the age of 62. The report was unfinished. Ironically, on the day of his death he became the first black chairman of the Congregational Union of England and Wales.

EDWARD ALLEYN

1566-1626

"IF I AM RICHER THAN MY ANCESTORS

I hope I may be able to do more good with my riches... that I was a player I cannot deny... My means of living were honest, and with the poor abilities wherewith God blessed me I was able to do something for myself, my relatives and my friends. Many of them now living at this day will not refuse to own what they owe to me. Therefore I am not ashamed."

The philanthropist, God-fearing founder of Dulwich College, Edward Alleyn, Churchwarden of St Saviour's Southwark, husband of the stepdaughter of the Dean of St Pauls, lived and worked for much of his life in the unruly Bankside area of Southwark. This was the Broadway of the Elizabethan stage and of William Shakespeare, which has today become holy ground for theatre lovers worldwide.

As a young man aged 21, at a time when the stage was a popular but unsavoury profession and performers were social outcasts, Edward Alleyn was the darling of Queen and public alike. With his devastating shrewdness and entrepreneurial skill, young Edward Alleyn was to carve for himself a respectable place in almost every aspect of Southwark's colourful life. Bear Master, brothel owner, banker, landlord, theatre manager and player, magistrate, art collector and property developer: he walked with saints and sinners.

In 1587 he played the lead in Christopher Marlowe's heroic play, *Tamburlaine*, written especially for his thundering voice and to raise the spirits of the nation at a time when England was threatened by the Spanish Armada. The two became friends and business partners, reading scripts and planning performances in the Southwark taverns. *Dr Faustus* and *The Jew of Malta* were also vehicles Marlowe created for his friend's talents.

Alleyn married well. His bride Joan Woodward was the step-daughter of Philip Henslowe, who owned the Rose Theatre, where the Admiral's Men performed. It was to prove a fortuitous relationship as Alleyn and Henslowe became business partners.

For the first year of their marriage, in 1593, Edward was on tour and the couple were separated. Joan was left in London where plague was raging. He wrote to her regularly and those letters are preserved at Dulwich College. They are touching in their tender detail.

What HAD she been up to!

"My good swete harte and loving mouse... I send thee a thousand comendations, wishing thee as well as well may be... But mouse, I littell thought to hear that which I now hear from you, for it is well knowne, they say, that you wear by lorde maior's officer mad to rid in a cart, you and all your felowes, which I ame sorry to hear: but you may thank your suporters, your stronge leges I mene, that would nott cary you away, but lett you fall into the hands of such Tarmagants. But mouse, when I com hom, I'll be revenged on 'em: tell then, mouse, I bid thee fayerwell... thyn ever, and nobodies els, by god of heaven."

Business activities started taking more of Alleyn's time. In 1594 he invested a considerable sum of money in the Bear Garden, which was situated in Paris Garden and which raised money for St Saviour's Church. Bear baiting was the hugely popular and profitable sport at the time, attended by The Queen and many visiting dignitaries. Ambassadors were taken to see the bears, who were each given fighting names such as Harry Hunks and Sarcason – much like wrestlers today.

Eventually, after King James 1 was crowned in 1603, Alleyn and Henslowe were granted their long awaited patents as Masters of the Bears.

In 1605, Alleyn bought the manor of Dulwich and some 1100 acres to which he and Joan moved several years later. But they were childless and Alleyn began to worry about the future of his now considerable estate. In 1613 he signed a contract with a bricklayer, John Benson, to build " a certain building of brick... which building shall be for a chapel, a schoolhouse and twelve almshouses". Pupils for the school, Alleyn's College of God's Gift, were to be drawn from the parishes of St Saviour and St Giles, Camberwell. But Alleyn had a grander vision still and in 1619 he was granted letters patent and was able to read the Deed of Foundation and statutes "to found a College in Dulwich to endure for ever..." before a distinguished gathering. Inigo Jones and Francis Bacon were among the company, who were treated to a banquet of over 100 items including pigeons, capon, beef, partridges, rabbits and oysters.

The College was to enrol 80 boys, including 12 poor scholars and "men children" of the inhabitants of Dulwich. They were to be educated freely but "forregners'" children were to pay. Alleyn laid down a complex set of statutes: the Master and warden were always to be of the founder's blood and name; "beef and mutton for the boys were to be sweete and good, their beer well brewed, their bread well baked; pupils were to wear coats of good cloth, of sad colour and lined". The almshouse inhabitants were to be responsible for keeping the grounds tidy and stocks were erected to punish any misbehaviour.

In 1623 Alleyn's wife died and was buried in the college chapel. Five months later he married Constance, daughter of John Donne, Dean of St Pauls. It is said that she brought three brothels in her marriage settlement and that she was 40 years his junior! The marriage was short-lived for in 1626 Edward Alleyn himself became ill and died. He left his wife just £100 of his great fortune and was buried, like Joan, in the College Chapel.

Dulwich College.

JOHN RUSKIN

1819-1900

A SAGE, with a PROFOUND AND PENETRATING INTELLECT, John Ruskin was one of the greatest of 19th century thinkers, acknowledged as the foremost art critic of his day when he was only 24.

The precocious only child of wealthy doting parents (his father was a prosperous wine merchant), he became the victim of too much over protective mother-love and quite unable to escape from the emotional cocoon of his rural childhood at 28 Herne Hill. A man of bewildering complexity, his innate love and appreciation of art and literature and his phenomenal literary creativity flourished amidst disorderly, unaesthetic surroundings with little apparent awareness of comfort or harmonious décor. His furniture was inherited old-fashioned jumble.

This brilliant, brooding and original mind – he was likened to an "elderly macaw picking at a bunch of grapes" – was tragically out of step with the inner emotional torment that dogged his adult life and eventually overwhelmed him. All his life he suffered from periods of acute depression.

His relations with women were disastrous. At 17 he was obsessed by Adele Domeq, daughter of his father's wine importing partner. The obsession came to nothing. His marriage to Effie Chalmers Grey was never consummated since he had a morbid fear of sex. So they divorced; his bizarre passion, when he was in his late fifties, for the mentally unsound teenager Rose LaTouche was ferociously contested by her parents and he remained blissfully oblivious to the passion for him nursed by social reformer Octavia Hill. When she was 15 years old he

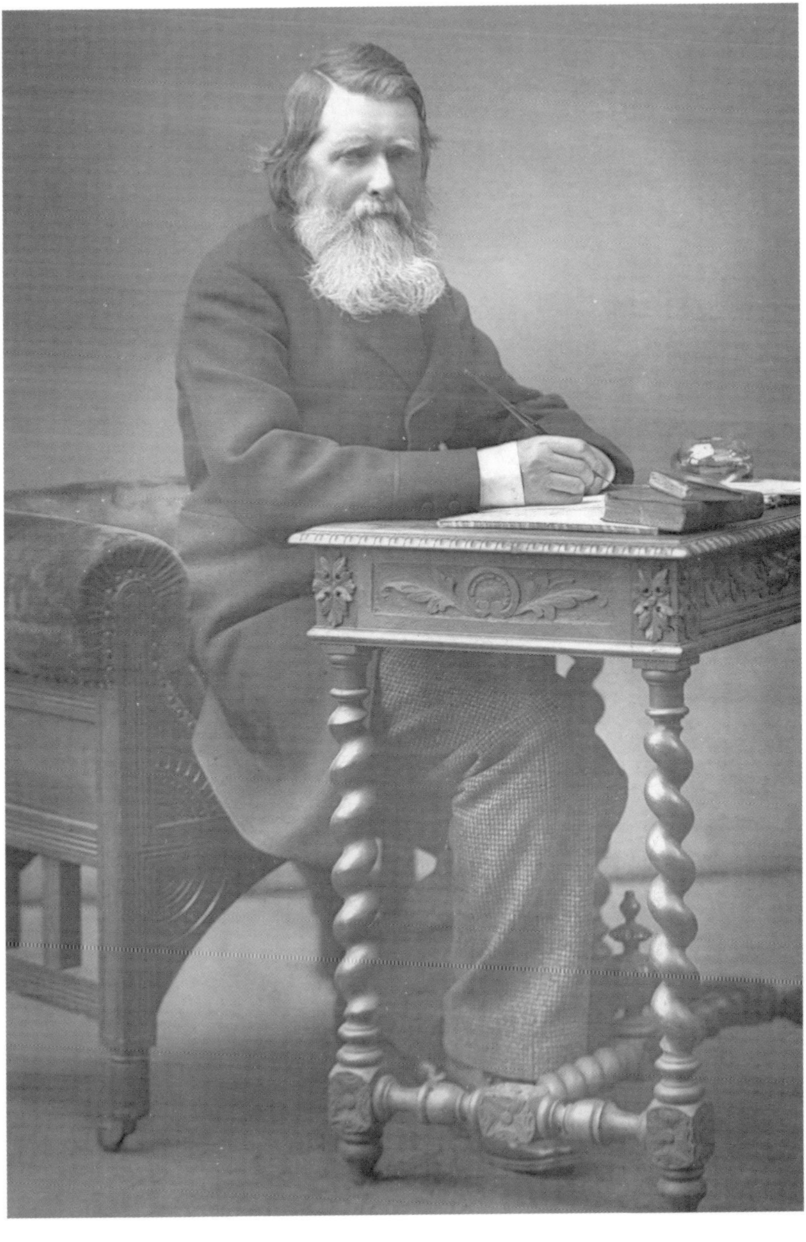

had volunteered to give her art lessons and she fell passionately in love with this wealthy, unattainable man. Too poor to afford carriage fares, she walked miles every day from central London, but Ruskin ignored her. Even so there is little doubt that he was the inspiration for her love of open spaces which was eventually to lead to the foundation of The National Trust.

Despite the family move in 1842 to a far more spacious, stylish house in seven acres of ground at Denmark Hill, Herne Hill was where John Ruskin always felt he belonged. However, the Ruskins retained the lease of the Herne Hill house and it was here that John stored his fine collection of mineral specimens, out of the way of his mother's tidiness.

When his father died in 1864, he left his son numerous properties, including Brantwood in the Lake District, a wonderful art collection and a fortune of £160,000; yet Ruskin remained living quietly alone with his mother.

The range of John Ruskin's work during those Dulwich years was admired the world over, even in Japan, a country which he had never visited. There his ideas influenced art, literature and politics and inspired the preservation of folk crafts. The Japanese Alpine Club was founded by men who had been moved by his descriptions of mountain landscapes.

Dulwich became an intellectual focus for men such as Thomas Carlyle, Charles Kingsley, Henry James, Lord Tennyson and the artists William Morris, Burne Jones and Holman Hunt.

Ruskin was a maverick, passionate about the dangers of industrial development to Europe's architectural heritage. He reminded the world that the most beautiful things, such as the peacock and the lily, are the most useless. "When we build, let us think we build for ever" he urged. His essay *On the Nature of Gothic* became the gospel of the developing Arts and Crafts Movement. He argued that the beauty of the Gothic style is marked by the joyful and creative work of its craftsmen, whereas much of Victorian style had been polluted by greed and commerce. Most of Ruskin's life was dominated by the writing of his massive four volume book *Modern Painters*.

Ruskin was also a dedicated admirer of contemporary landscape artists at a time when critics were accusing Turner, in particular, of defying nature. Contrarily Ruskin claimed that Turner was the first painter in all history to have given an entire transcript of nature.

In 1869 he was elected the first Slade Professor of Fine Arts at Oxford and then, in 1871, his mother died. That year he suffered a stroke and severe depression. Bereavement and the ugly deterioration of the countryside around Dulwich made him decide to uproot and move to the Lake District.

He gave the Herne Hill house as a wedding present to his cousin Joanna Agnew. But although the countryside around was fast disappearing under urban sprawl, and the childhood rural idyll was no more, he could not, even then, sever the link, insisting that he should be allowed to turn his former nursery into a study, for use whenever he was in London. Here he started work on an autobiography, *Praeterita*. Ruskin last visited the house in 1888 but the beauty of the Lake District did not bring him the inner peace he longed for. The bouts of depression and then madness increased, and for the 10 years before he died John Ruskin was not capable of writing anything other than his name... but his influence had been great. In 1906 when the first Labour MPs in Parliament were asked to name the writers who had influenced them most, John Ruskin was top of the list.

ROBERT BROWNING

1812-1889

OH TO BE IN ENGLAND
Now that April's there,
And whoever wakes in England,
Sees some morning unaware
That the lowest boughs and the brushwood sheaf
Round the elm tree base, are in tiny leaf,
While the chaffinch sings on the orchard bough.
In England – now!

Robert Browning's famous poem *Home thoughts from Abroad*, written in 1845, reflects a painfully nostalgic yearning for the countryside of his childhood around Peckham and Camberwell. How beautiful and exciting it all was for a child with a passion for small animals, nature and poetry.

"I used to lie in the grass on Camberwell's hills and watch the world go by."

Browning was born in the spring of 1812 at Rainbow Cottage, on Cottage Green, Camberwell – a house with some 6,000 books. From its windows were views across fields as far as the Strand in central London. Dulwich was a "green half hour's walk away" where Robert loved to visit the magnificent art gallery recently designed by Sir John Soane, although he admitted that he was under age at the time. In the summer he lay for hours dreaming among the Camberwell elms and in the autumn gypsies flocked to a fair on Camberwell Green.

The little boy was greatly influenced by his mother who, a member of York Street Congregational Church in Walworth, was a devout Christian of whom it was said "she was one of those people who have no need to go to Heaven – they make it wherever they are". One of young Robert's favourite games was to dress up as a minister and stand on a chair to preach to his bewildered little sister Sarianna!

Before he was five years old Robert was painting (with redcurrant juice) and writing poetry. His father, a kindly, learned, but surprisingly modern bibliophile, encouraged the boy's curiosity about books through imaginative play. Robert recalled later in a poem *Development* written in 1888, the year before he died, how, when he asked his father about the Siege of Troy, Mr Browning brought it dramatically to life by piling up chairs on the table, to represent the city, Robert was to play Priam, the cat was Helen and the dogs took the part of Agamemnon and Menelaus.

Throughout his childhood Browning wrote poems. His parents tried, unsuccessfully to have them published and later Browning himself destroyed them all. He was always an intensely private person.

He was enrolled in a nearby elementary school but he was too bright and so, at the age of eight, he was sent in his dark brown uniform to be a weekly boarder at the Misses Readys' Collegiate School in Peckham. Eventually, it was said, "time healed the pain of the endless weekly partings but not the intense dislike of the school".

There he stayed until he was 14, growing increasingly confident and self-centred. He was wilful and insubordinate. His father taught him Latin and Greek but it was the gift from his cousin of a book of Percy Bysshe Shelley's poems that focussed his thinking and changed the direction of his life. He became a vegetarian and an atheist and decided to become a poet. In 1828 the University of London was opened and since there were no religious requirements for entry, unlike Oxford or Cambridge, Browning enrolled.

For Browning, Edmund Kean's performance of *Richard III* was worth the effort of a 20 mile walk from Camberwell. He was overwhelmed, and decided to write a poem, an opera and a novel, in such a way that no one would realise they were by the same author. By 1833 he had written *Pamela* – an anonymous but autobiographical work for which his aunt paid the publication costs.

The following year he was appointed "secretary" to the Consul General in Moscow, travelling with him around Russia. On his return to Peckham he wrote *How They Brought the Good News from Ghent to Aix* and *Ivan Ivanovitch*, inspired by the journey. His literary output was, by now, prodigious and his reputation growing.

In December 1840 the Brownings decided that their Camberwell home was not large enough and so they moved to New Cross. Here Robert buried himself in a study where he kept a notorious pet spider, housed on his desk in a human skull. In 1841 he produced *Pippa Passes*, his first memorable major work. He was only 29. *My Last Duchess* followed and then *The Pied Piper of Hamelin*.

1844 was the next milestone in Browning's life. He had read and admired the poetry of Elizabeth Barrett and a year later, in May, they met and embarked on a now famous, daily flood of letters. These letters were at first restrained "Dear Mr Browning" and "Dear Miss Barrett" but by August she had become "my own dearest love". They exchanged lockets and locks of hair and over the next two years had created in their correspondence a frank and full picture of mid-19th century life, fashions, friends, ideas and emotions.

It was an unlikely romance. Elizabeth was six years older than Robert and had aged beyond her years due to lifelong illness. But when her father decided the family should move from Wimpole Street the couple escaped and married secretly in Marylebone – she was so excited she could barely sign the register. In 1846 Elizabeth Barrett Browning and Robert left England for their new home in Italy. But exhaustion brought on by the journey and then the summer heat was to prove too much. She died quietly in his arms on June 29th and was buried in the Protestant Cemetery in Florence. Browning returned to England and lived, writing prolifically, until 1889 dying, like his beloved Elizabeth, while on a journey to Italy, where he hoped to be buried. But such was his fame that his body was returned in great style to London, where he was buried in Westminster Abbey.

ELEPHANT AND CASTLE
AND AROUND THE BOROUGH

The Elephant and Castle, c.1905.

RICHARD CUMING

1777-1870

ON RICHARD CUMING'S FIFTH BIRTHDAY Mrs Coleman of Manor Place in Walworth gave him the fossil of a sea lily and a Mogul coin. She generated in the little boy the spark which was to fire a lifelong passion for collecting, which later led to the foundation of the extraordinary Cuming Museum.

Today the museum, in Walworth Road, brims over with items reflecting Richard Cuming's obsession with the curiosities of life. For Southwark, in particular, it tells the story of the borough seen through hundreds of archaeological and historical discoveries.

Richard Cuming was the second son of Richard Cuming and Lady Martha Maxwell. His elder brother, John Brompton Cuming, became a landscape artist and Royal Academician, painting many scenes of the borough of Southwark.

As a little boy, living in 3 Deans Row (now 196 Walworth Road) Richard made himself a cardboard cabinet for his growing collection: "eight drawers being devoted to minerals and fossils and two deep boxes at the top for coins and other trifles".

He always rose at 4am and, whenever possible, would escape to the country around Walworth, taking with him a simple meal. There he sketched and collected specimens of nature, also painting pictures of rural Walworth and Kennington. He was an inventive boy. In 1792 he made a microscope from sliding tubes of cardboard, a mahogany stand and thin plates of micah instead of glass. The following year he made a "phantasmagoria" – a magic lantern. His subject was the ghost of a nun, who by mechanical means he made to look right and left, with a dagger pointing to her wounded bosom.

As a man Richard Cuming never tried to make any money from his ideas. He hated ostentation; he was neat in dress, wearing only one gold family ring, which bore the motto "God be our Guide". Pious, cheery, he was very popular and hospitable to his friends, who included a galaxy of men of letters. Nothing pleased him better than to share his curios with them. He became one of the first members of the Entomological Society of London.

When the Leverian Museum on Blackfriars Road was sold in 1806, Richard Cuming bought many of its curios. Piles from lake dwellings, relics from the days when Southwark was a swamp; flints; foreign paraphernalia; a Ram's Horn, used by the Southwark Jews before they were expelled from England in 1290; a sheep's heart stuck with pins; a piece of cork with a farthing embedded as a fisherman's bribe to the sea Gods; and the lace mittens worn by baby Charles I at his christening: all these were crammed into his home in Walworth Road.

When the old man died, in 1870 at the age of 92, his son, Henry Syer Cuming, took over. On his death in 1902, he left the entire collection, plus money to fund its upkeep, to the Borough of Southwark: so was the well-loved Cuming Museum created, an exuberant memorial to a man who loved life.

CHARLES CHAPLIN

1889-1977

Charlie Chaplin, MULTI-MILLIONAIRE STAR of THE SILENT SCREEN, drew inspiration for many of his films from the characters who lived and worked in the Southwark slums of his childhood.

The films *The Kid* and *Easy Street* are based on Charlie's memories of that time, running wild in ragged, dirty clothes, amongst sordid, murky alleys and market debris around the Walworth Road.

When he died in 1977, *The Times* eulogised "he achieved greater, more widespread fame in his own lifetime than perhaps anyone else in the world".

Sir Charles Spencer Chaplin, as he became, was the son of Charles Chaplin, a comedian, and Hannah Harriet Hill, from Walworth, a music hall soubrette with gypsy blood and the stage name of Lily Harley. His parents separated a year after he was born, leaving Hannah to support young Charles and his elder half-brother Sydney.

Mrs Harriet Tricks, who was present at Charlie's birth, said later: "he had a hard life as a child. He used to curl up in the doorway of Mr Wentworth, the lamp manufacturer in Kennington Road." Mrs Tricks used to take him bread and butter and tea, after charring at Mr Wentworth's. He was, she said, even then, a mischievous boy, full of tricks, tripping himself up, climbing fences and falling off.

In an interview with the *Daily Herald* in 1952 Chaplin said " I shall always remember the top room where I lived as a boy. I remember how I had to climb up and down three flights of narrow stairs to empty the buckets of troublesome slops." On a Saturday the two boys wandered

Below: The Charlie Chaplin public house.

through The Cut, peering hungrily into the cook shop windows at the tantalising, steaming roast joints they could not afford.

Much of the boys' early time was spent in Lambeth Workhouse because Hannah could not cope and was sent to Cane Hill Asylum. "I didn't cry" he recalled "but a baffling despair overcame me". He roamed the streets trying to find enough to keep himself alive and even then dreamed of himself as the greatest actor in the world. He adored his mother. He recalled that, sometimes, in the early days, when she knew she would be late home from the theatre, she left their favourite Neopolitan cake on the table, for the boys to find in the morning.

They had a fragmented education, with more truancy than schooling. "Education bewildered me with facts in which I was only mildly interested" he admitted. His first teacher always claimed that the famous Chaplin walk was evolved in those days and was copied from an old man who gave oats and water to the horses at the Elephant and Castle.

When Charlie was eight years old, he and his brother went to live with the father they had never known. He lived in Kennington Park Road, with his mistress. The couple drank heavily and Charlie said, in his autobiography, years later "It was a gruesomely sad house." Life became increasingly depressing. He wrote then: "I hear the lively music of the concertina passing by the back bedroom window, playing a Highland march, accompanied by rowdy youths and giggling coster girls. The vigour and vitality of it seemed ruthlessly indifferent to my unhappiness."

When his mother returned from the asylum and went to collect the boys she was "still the same sweet smiling mother" and they rejoined her for a while. Charlie became a waif of the streets, left to his own devices and wandering through the squalid Southwark slums.

Charlie's father died from dropsy in St Thomas's Hospital in 1899. He was only 37. The coffin was lined with white satin and Charlie recalled that there were white daisies placed around his face. They were from his father's mistress. "It was macabre and horrifying." His frail mother, ground down by poverty, returned to the asylum.

In his autobiography Charles claims that his first public appearance was at the age of five. On stage his mother's voice cracked and became a whisper. Charles was asked by the stage manager to replace her and led the little boy forward "on the stage alone... before a glare of footlights and faces in smoke I started to sing... a well known song called 'Jack Jones'... halfway through money was showered on stage." He decided to pick up the money and continue the song afterwards. The stage manager came and helped but Charles was worried he planned to keep it. "This thought conveyed itself to the audience who laughed even more." Only when the stage manager handed the money to his mother did Charles return to finish the song. This was his theatrical debut – and his mother's final appearance.

At the age of nine Charles was given his first professional job. He was a clog dancer, wearing knickerbockers, with The Eight Lancashire Lads (one of which was a girl) at The Montpellier in Walworth Road. Clog dancing bored him. He longed to perform solos and double acts and to play the villain in a real drama.

He dabbled in a succession of jobs. He was a glass blower, news vendor, a toymaker and a printer. For a time he joined some woodcutters in Kennington Park Road. Then one day he was given a present that was to change his life – a twopenny gallery seat for Fred Karno's comedy, *Early Birds*, in which brother Sydney was already playing. That night fuelled the ambitious fires that were eventually to take him to Hollywood.

By the time he was 11 years old Charlie was appearing in music hall all over the country and pestering agents.

At 17, sporting the great red nose and cane for which he later became so famous, he was top of the bill. He was a riotous success at the London Coliseum in *The Football Match*, swaggering on and hitting himself on the side of the head, till his trousers fell down. Walking home that night he stopped for a celebration cup of tea, at a stall by the Elephant and Castle, near the pub that today bears his name.

In 1908, he finally met the celebrated Fred Karno at The Fun Factory in Vaughan Road, Camberwell. Karno remembered him as a "puny, sullen looking youngster." But he joined the troupe at £3 10s a week, playing all the local theatres – The South London Palace, Camberwell Palace and the Peckham Hippodrome. It was with Fred Karno that he learned his craft. By 1910 he was off to America to fulfil that childhood dream of becoming the "greatest actor in the world."

But Charlie never forgot his mother and years later, when she was mentally unsound, he arranged for her to leave London and go to live in America where he and Sydney had settled.

Charlie Chaplin eventually married actress Oona O'Neil and left America, a victim of McCarthyism, to make his home in Switzerland with their eight children until he died in 1977.

JOHN HARVARD

1607-1638

AMERICA'S OLDEST UNIVERSITY was founded with a legacy from a young English Puritan, John Harvard, who had fled from Southwark to escape religious unrest. When he died he left a fortune and a library of over 300 books, to "advance learning and perpetuate it to posterity".

John Harvard was born in 1607, son of a prosperous "flesh monger", or butcher, in Borough High Street and his wife, Katherine, "a woman of sincere piety". She had grown up with William Shakespeare's brother Edmund, in Stratford-upon-Avon. John was baptised in St Saviour's Church (now Southwark Cathedral.)

Seven year old John was at his desk by seven every morning in St Saviour's Grammar School, where his father was a governor. In his satchel were a Bible and a supply of "good candles for the dark hours". On the way he would have seen the heads of those who had fallen foul of the law, atop the 18 poles that stood at the entrance to London Bridge. He learned grammar, oratory, poetry, Greek and Hebrew. In the weekly break for play no pupil was allowed to play games for money but they could leap or run and wrestle or shoot with a long bow or play chess as much as they liked. There were only two short breaks a year.

John's father had gained a position of considerable importance at St Saviour's Church and the family worshipped there together on Sundays. In 1625, the Harvards' secure and warm family life was shattered by the plague. John was devastated by the death of four brothers and his father Robert; only his mother, and brother Thomas survived. Katherine remarried almost immediately, only to be widowed again and so inherit a second considerable legacy.

Statue of John Harvard outside Harvard University in the United States.

John decided to enter the church and went to that bastion of Puritanism, Emmanuel College, Cambridge. He was there for seven years, returning home eventually, ordained, to find his mother was dead and already buried in St Saviour's Church. She left her fortune to be shared between John and his brother. In addition there was The Queen's Head Inn, in Borough High Street, which she had bought and left to John as an investment.

He spent much of that summer with friends at the country vicarage at Ringmer, in Sussex; there he courted the vicar's daughter, Ann Sadler. They were married in April 1636.

John was now in a financial position to indulge his love of learning. He had been collecting books, especially on theology, but became increasingly concerned by the religious unrest which was to lead eventually to the Civil War.

Early in 1637 he packed up his treasured books and emigrated with Ann to Charleston, New England, where he quickly won a reputation as "a godly gentleman and a lover of learning". In the same year his beloved brother died in Southwark, leaving everything to John.

The journey and the new life in America took their toll of his health and in 1638, just one year after landing, he died. He left all his library and half his now considerable estate towards the building of a University at Cambridge in Massachusetts: an act which was described as a "union between private munificence and public education."

Southwark remembers him with a library in his name, and a stained glass window in the Harvard Chapel of Southwark Cathedral. It was unveiled by the American donor, Ambassador Joseph H. Choate, in 1905. He said "the name of John Harvard, unknown and of little account when he left England, has been a benediction to the New World and his timely and generous act has borne fruit a millionfold."

THOMAS GUY

1644-1724

PHILANTHROPIST Thomas Guy, founder of one of London's finest teaching hospitals and UNSTINTING BENEFACTOR of Southwark's poor, left no letters or diary. His careless, scruffy appearance and habit of dining on his printing shop counter with no more than newspaper for a cloth, led to totally unfounded rumours of meanness.

Thomas Guy was born in Horsleydown, Southwark, less than a mile from the site of the hospital he was to found. He inherited from his Anabaptist father a fairly serious, thoughtful disposition.

In 1668 he was admitted as Freeman of the Stationers' Company. By this time he had become a sharp, quick-witted businessman with a bookshop and publishing company opposite the Mansion House and, having invested wisely, became immensely wealthy.

Deeds were always more important than words for him. Guy was a man of genuine compassion whose heart was particularly touched by the plight of women and who preferred to help, quietly, wherever he saw there was need.

By 1695 Thomas Guy was an MP. In 1694 he had been invited to become a Sheriff of London, an appointment which would have led to his being elected Lord Mayor. He declined, on account, it is said, of the expense involved. Pomp and ceremony did not appeal. Rumours arose, and malicious stories of his parsimony were spread at a time when, ironically, Guy was quietly giving his fortune away.

Thomas Guy discussing plans for Guy's Hospital with the architect.

In 1704 he was asked to serve as a Governor of St Thomas's Hospital, Southwark, which was in dire need of repair and generous benefactors. He gave large amounts of money for capital projects. Thomas Guy was a careful, cautious man but always sensitive to the immediate problems of patients, especially those who could not work when discharged from hospital. He donated £100 a year to help them. He also established a fund which could be diverted to the needy and provide for the 1,400 Protestant refugees from Europe, living in insanitary tents and warehouses in the area. He continued for the rest of his life to be alert and to respond financially to the needs of the poor.

He was generous, too, to his own relatives who were in distress, bailing debtors out of the Marshalsea Prison. He also astutely, and on a grand scale, lent money with interest to the nobility. Despite all this, the stories rumbled on and his cautious prudence was misunderstood.

Early in 1721, the records of St Thomas's Hospital note the first formal arrangement about a new hospital. "Our worthy governor and benefactor, Thomas Guy, intending to found and erect an Hospital for Incurables, in the close of this Hospital... we have agreed to grant him a lease..." On March 1st it was noted "our worthy benefactor, Thomas Guy, having desired a small piece of garden, late Norgate's – for his new Hospital – granted."

The remainder of Thomas Guy's life was spent supervising the building of his hospital. The foundations were laid in the Spring of 1722 and work progressed at such breakneck speed that the fabric was roofed before he died, on 27 December 1724. He was 80 years old. Little more than a week later the new Guy's Hospital was opened and in January 1725 the first sixty patients were admitted.

On his death, his executors found a chest containing one thousand guineas which they used to pay for a very elaborate funeral of forty coaches, with six horses apiece. His body lay in state in Mercers' Hall, Cheapside and was then interred in the parish church of St Thomas, Southwark. 200 Blue Coat boys from Christ's Hospital walked, singing, before the hearse. A plaster cast of his face was given to the hospital to perpetuate his memory and later, in 1780, a monument was erected over his remains.

CHARLES DICKENS

1812-1870

DICKENS' OBSESSIONS with the DEGRADATION of London's poor and the intolerable conditions in the prisons were formed during his own desperately unhappy youth. As a small boy he had lived what he described later as an "idyllic" existence in the countryside of Rochester in Kent. Then, just before Charles' 11th birthday, his father, a pay clerk at Chatham Docks, found himself in financial difficulties and the family moved to London.

Charles spent his time wandering the streets. A year later his sister, Fanny, won a scholarship and became a boarder at The Royal Academy of Music. Charles, to his eternal shame, was found work.

As a sensitive, middle-class boy of twelve, with an educated accent, Charles found himself labouring amongst working-class boys at Warren's "forlorn, dirty, ramshackle" boot-blacking factory. It was at the foot of Hungerford Stairs, on the north side of the Thames, where Charing Cross Station now stands. The dreadful cruelty of the river preyed on his mind. To him it was "a place of death".

Within two weeks of starting work in the blacking factory Charles' father was arrested for debt and taken to the Marshalsea Debtors' prison in Southwark.

This was a terrible place; dank, overcrowded, insanitary and degrading, surrounded by the high wall some of which can still be seen today.

Rooms were, on average, 8ft by 12ft. Charles never forgot the two bricks in his father's grate, there to prevent the fire from burning too quickly. "With swollen eyes and through shining tears" the distressed boy ran around the gloomy, grimy streets of The Borough, trying desperately and vainly to raise the money to secure his father's release.

At ten every evening a bell rang to warn visitors the prison was closing and young Charles would creep out into Borough High Street. "The busy sounds of traffic resound in it from morn to midnight, but the streets around are mean and close: poverty and debauchery lie festering in the crowded alleys, want and misfortune are pent up in the narrow prison: an air of gloom and dreariness seems... to hang about the scene and impart to it, a squalid and sickly hue."

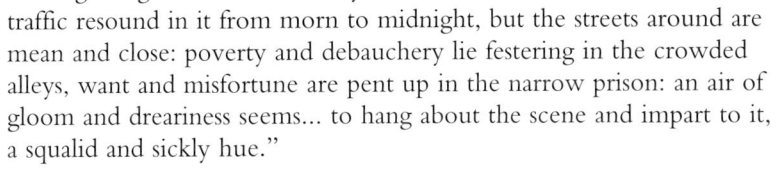

Meanwhile, Mrs Dickens struggled on, gradually selling all the family possessions until, in shame, the entire family, except Charles and Fanny, moved in to the Marshalsea too.

On Sundays Charles went to collect Fanny from the Academy and together they walked to visit their family. Amid more tears, Charles confided to his father about his desperate loneliness. New lodgings were found for him in Lant Street, near the prison, in the house of an Insolvent Court agent. It was two minutes' walk from the Marshalsea and Charles thought the lodgings was paradise. He wrote:

"Lant Street was colonised by a few clear-starchers, a sprinkling of journeymen bookbinders, one or two prison agents for the Insolvent Court, several small housekeepers who are employed in the Docks, a handful of mantua makers and a seasoning of jobbing tailors. The majority of inhabitants either direct their energies to the letting of furnished apartments, or devote themselves to the healthful and invigorating pursuit of mangling. The chief features in the still life of the streets, are green shutters, lodging bills, brass door-plates and bell-handles: the principal specimens of animated nature, the pot boy, the muffin youth, the baked-potato man. The population is migratory, usually disappearing on the verge of quarter-day and generally by night. His Majesty's revenues are seldom collected in this happy valley, the rents are dubious, and water communication very frequently cut off."

Every morning he would breakfast with his parents before setting out for the blacking factory. Twelve hours later, exhausted, he returned over Blackfriars Bridge, towards Great Suffolk Street, to join the family for supper in the Marshalsea. Today the streets are named after the characters he created: Pickwick Street, Little Dorrit Court, Quilp Street. In Lant Street, where he lived, is the Charles Dickens Primary School.

Charles' father inherited money which cleared his debt and he was released on 28th May. The entire family were able to move to Hampstead and Charles went back to school. This dark and miserable time of Dickens' young life, in Southwark, which later so deeply influenced many of his greatest novels, was at an end.

THE EAST FAMILY
and THE GEORGE INN

THE NEAR-LEGENDARY East family was linked with The George Inn, Borough High Street, for over 170 years.

John East 1762-1822

The story begins in the late 18th century when grandfather John East ran a prosperous haulage service from the notorious Jacob's Island area of Bermondsey. His broad-wheeled waggons pulled by four horses, their harness gleaming, were a fine and familiar sight in Borough High Street and along Bankside. John East himself was an imposing figure, in his frock coat with flowers in his button hole and striped weskit.

In those days Borough High Street was an almost continuous ale house serving the busy commercial life of Southwark. Everyone danced attendance on John East – he was a good customer. Often he stayed overnight at the centuries-old George Inn, in his own personal four-poster bed. As a successful and respected patron and a sparkling raconteur, he expected, and received, exceptional treatment.

John East married in 1798 and his son, John James, was born the following year. In 1809 he leased stabling for his horses from the landlord of The George and the family moved in to an apartment at the Inn. So began the long business association.

John James East 1799-1878

When John East died his son John James took over. But the opening of the new London Bridge in 1831 and building of London Bridge station in 1844 badly affected the carriage business.

On occasion Charles Dickens was known to divide his time between the Trafalgar at Greenwich and The George at Southwark which was just as Dickens had described it in Pickwick Papers. It has hardly changed today.

John James eventually returned to live, for a time, in Greenwich to bring up his son Charles (1835-1862) and his adopted little girls, Amelia and Elisabeth. Charles and Elisabeth fell in love and married but Charles died, at the age of 27, leaving two sons, John Marlborough and Charles Alexander East. John James decided that the boys must go to boarding school. When they returned two years later everything had changed: their aunt Amelia and her two children were permanently installed at The George. Amelia, like their mother a widow, had long before accepted the tyrannical demands of John James as head of the family. She lived, with her children Agnes and Frederick, in the lap of luxury as his housekeeper. First Amelia and then her daughter ruled The George with a rod of iron for 60 years.

John Marlborough East 1860-1924
Charles Alexander East 1863-1914

After the boys left boarding school, Charles trained at The George to become a licensed victualler. John Marlborough was apprenticed to a glass artist.

At the age of 14 John was already 6'3" tall and was often humiliated by the brutal old man's treatment. One night, having been horse-whipped for spilling a mug of beer, he made up his mind to run away. He packed his artists materials, his canvasses and twelve gold sovereigns from a secret hidey-hole beside the fireplace and, as the old Parliament clock struck four, he crept out into the bitter wind of Borough High Street.

For a time the boy earned a living as best he could, modelling and painting. Eventually he found himself on the stage and from then on never looked back. He became a star of touring melodrama and pantomime offering "blood and thunder at the people's prices."

When John first left home, young Charles was left to his own devices at The George until the manager of the Greenwich Theatre suggested that he, too, might appear in panto. His first role was as an onion! But the taste for acting was established and ultimately Charles followed in his brother's footsteps. His grandfather died in 1878 and Amelia immediately took over as landlady.

Charles Alexander East

In 1893 the East brothers "came home" to Southwark. John took over as manager of the South London Palace, whose reputation for star turns had spread far beyond the Elephant and Castle and was affectionately known as the "Shrine of the South." Electricity had just been installed in the theatre. It was, said the brochure, "both chaste and elegant, delicate and beautiful, which gives the interior a glow of oriental splendour."

John East was a master showman. One of his best remembered stunts promoted a show called Hypnotism Exposed, featuring "Professor" Dale. A hearse was to be driven nightly along the Walworth Road, carrying two coffins which contained the unconscious bodies of the "Professor's" two assistants.

In tandem with the Palace, John East ran the Lyric Hammersmith. In 1900 he produced his first play for the Elephant and Castle Theatre, then near to the present Elephant and Castle main line station. The Elephant flourished in an area where the scent of leather, oysters and horses prevailed. It accommodated more than 1,000 people – mostly dedicated to blood and thunder, beer and chips. Charles East was the star turn playing in such heart-wringing dramas as East Lynne with its unforgettable line "Dead, dead and never called me mother!".

The two brothers dominated the South London theatre scene until, in 1907, there was a downfall in takings. Cheaper transport took crowds away from Southwark "up west" and new picture palaces were drawing audiences.

Amelia East 1827-1903
and Agnes East 1853-1934

Meanwhile Agnes had taken over The George in 1903, when her mother died in the bed that had always been hers. A handsome, commanding woman she always took time to sit with her customers and yarn about the old days and could recite Dickens' descriptions of her home by heart. She was immensely proud of the inn's former famous client and eagerly showed visitors his table by the window saying "I should have loved to have met Mr Dickens". She expected visitors to arrive carrying a copy of *Pickwick Papers* so that she could conduct them on a tour of her home. She changed nothing: the mysterious corridors, the attics thick with the grime of centuries, shelves crowded with pewter pots and silverware, which had been in constant use since the East family first set up there in 1809. The four-poster bed with its mounting block remained, the rag rugs, the rocking chair. The old Parliament clock in the coffee room ticked away the 19th and the 20th centuries just as it is ticking away today. Agnes herself was as unchanging as her surroundings. Her own sitting room was a haven from the hubbub outside, crammed with antiques and curios, photographs and prints.

In the coffee room she kept a black parrot called Jackie which had been bought for her in Silver Street market. Jackie became famous for his silence. Agnes always refused to abandon her silent parrot – "a parrot that can't talk is the talk of the town" she said.

As she grew older Agnes discouraged visitors from staying at The George, although the four-poster was always made up with fresh linen. Since she liked to retire early to bed, late arrivals often found the fire in the coffee room disconcertingly dead. Until 1934 there was no electricity and no telephone at The George. Nor was there a bathroom – only a hip bath – and four jugs of water!

"We've never catered specifically for sightseers, only the travellers and merchants of Southwark. They've eaten our mutton for five centuries. It's no place for ladies", Agnes proudly declared.

She lived to see her beloved home in the brochures of many travel guides, and though she greeted her foreign visitors and the famous who now favoured her table with a quiet smile, she would tolerate no nonsense. On one occasion, when Winston Churchill arrived with a bottle of his favourite port, she charged him corkage!

She died in 1934 at the age of eighty one, leaving nothing at all to any of the East family.

CAPTAIN EYRE MASSEY SHAW

1828-1908

"OH CAPTAIN SHAW!
Type of true love kept under!
Could thy brigade, with cold cascade
Quench my great love, I wonder?"

When this lyric was sung at the first performance of Gilbert and Sullivan's operetta *Iolanthe*, in 1882, it immortalised the charms of Captain Eyre Massey Shaw. He was a flamboyant character, whose fire-fighting reforms and courage were honoured throughout Britain and the world.

Captain Shaw accepted the post of Superintendent in the London Fire Engine Establishment in 1861. He succeeded the legendary James Braidwood, creator of the Establishment, who was killed in the great Tooley Street fire. Shaw was only 34 years old and married to Anna Maria with four children.

It was a time of great fire danger for London residents. The risks were increasing due to the invention of the phosphorus friction match, paraffin oil lamps and women's new full flowing skirts. Planning controls did not exist and the gas lighting of narrow streets, bounded by overcrowded houses and ever taller buildings, made fires inevitable and often devastating.

Within six months Captain Shaw had submitted evidence to the House of Commons, showing the urgent need for radical reform. During his lifetime he transformed the service with the inauguration of the London-wide Metropolitan Fire Brigade in 1866.

He approached his task with military efficiency, insisting on discipline at all times. For this reason his recruits were all former sailors. He believed that only men accustomed to life at sea would instantly obey orders, be handy and practical and could cope with the long, irregular hours and night watches. They called him "The Skipper". He was tough, brusque and often rude but they admired him to a man, because he never shirked danger, was always with them on a job and was injured many times.

He was also always very hard on the dozens of enthusiastic but inefficient and unruly volunteer forces that "come when they like, amuse themselves, and go when they like."

Special helmets were issued by the Board of Trade at Shaw's insistence, so that the volunteers could be recognised and by 1877 they had been re-formed on a respectable, reliable footing.

Captain Shaw loved travel and journeyed all over the world, studying the fire-fighting services in foreign parts. As a result he was a prolific writer of books and pamphlets, forcefully propounding his knowledge and ideas. In 1868 his 53 page *Instructions for the Use and Management of Fire Escapes and Rescue of Life from Fire* insisted that, to prevent panic, a fireman could use force "...nothing can exceed the disgrace of men rushing wildly out to save themselves and leaving helpless women and children to perish in the flames."

But perhaps one of his greatest contributions to the fire service was his book *Fires in Theatres* in which he reported on the safety of each of London's 41 theatres. It was the most massive administrative task of his life resulting in a 370 page report.

In the late 19th century fire-fighting had become an upper class pastime. Royalty and aristocrats liked nothing better than to watch a good fire, or to play at fire-fighters. The Prince of Wales, the Duke of Sutherland and the Earl of Caithness, each had his own uniform and regularly attended blazes. By the time that the new London headquarters had been opened at Winchester House in Southwark Bridge Road in 1878, there was a regular weekly outing of aristocratic ladies and gentlemen to stand on the balcony of Captain and Mrs Shaw's house, to watch the fire-fighting excitements laid on for their entertainment.

The new Brigade headquarters also provided a spacious, elegant new home in Southwark for the Shaws and their six children. Converted from two town houses, the property lay in an extensive site which had been part of the former Winchester Park estate. It had eight bedrooms, a large dining room and a drawing room in which there was a statue of Captain Shaw by Count Gleichen – "to The Extinguisher from some of his chums." In the same complex was a block with 83 rooms, which housed four superintendents and provided a waiting room, watch room and lecture room.

Inside was entirely appropriate for exalted company. Outside was a different matter. The Mint, which surrounded it, was still one of London's roughest areas. The walls had to be raised to 15ft and topped with glass in order to prevent rubbish and excrement from being thrown over. The gateways were used as a urinal and the noise and stench from the nearby public houses were unbearable. None of this seemed to deter the Prince and his friends.

The Shaws' social life became more and more sparkling. They were guests of the Royal Family at Sandringham and Captain Shaw organised a number of special events to please the Prince of Wales's visiting dignitaries. The Prince's secretary wrote on one occasion in 1878: " The Prince of Wales desires me to thank you for your letter. He thinks your programme a capital one but would prefer a good fire to seeing the printing of The Daily Telegraph. Could you not get one up for him on purpose!"

Sadly, Captain Shaw was not a family man. He had a reputation as a womaniser. He had no time to spare for his children and his professional and personal lifestyle meant that Anna Maria was often left alone to organise "at homes" and perform charitable works.

Shaw slept in his own room, from which Mrs Shaw was excluded. There he lined up a regiment of uniforms to change into after each soaking. On the floor were a row of jackboots "standing erect.... like a well drilled regiment". He also installed a speaking tube above his bed and in every part of the house, so that he could be reached at a moment's notice. He always rose early to drill the men, wrote and received reports in the morning and then travelled up to forty miles to inspect his men further afield. Sometimes he made spot checks unannounced. His energy was formidable.

Only at Christmas did the house ring with the sounds of family life. Then the Shaws donated generously to the huge festivities, spread over three evenings, one of which was set aside for the children, when 300 toys were distributed. There were sweets, music and dancing for all the brigade and their friends.

He resigned on 31 October 1891 and was knighted on his last day of service.

THE FIRE DOGS of SOUTHWARK

DO DOGS HAVE GHOSTS? The mysterious and heartwarming story of the fire dogs of Southwark was believed by many people in the 19th century to prove that the spirit of an animal may live on and reappear from time to time.

On 22 June 1861 one of Southwark's worst fires began amongst the hemp at Stovell's warehouse overlooking Tooley Street. At that time London's fire brigade chief was the celebrated James Braidwood. Although the brigade arrived within a few minutes, the whole place was ablaze and spreading fast. Crowds on London Bridge watched, aghast, as men who rowed out to try and salvage the 10,000 casks of melted tallow floating in the river were burned to death.

Braidwood, a courageous and unflappable man, was there in person. Hurrying along Tooley Street he was tragically buried beneath a collapsing wall of red hot bricks. Later, from nowhere, a dark brown dog appeared. It seemed to be a bull terrier mastiff cross and had shining saucer-like eyes. Barking and pulling at fireman Robert Tozer's coat, it led him exactly to where the charred body of James Braidwood lay, completely hidden from view.

James Braidwood

The fire-fighters believed that this was the ghost of the bull terrier cross named Chance, which had turned up out of the blue and attached himself to the Watling Street fire station, in 1834. Chance had raced the fire engines back and forth and had died, a hero, in a blaze.

Even more curious, 21 years after the Tooley Street fire, Robert Tozer's son Dick was fighting a fire in Fleet Street, across the river, under the command of James Braidwood's successor, Captain Shaw. Suddenly, from nowhere, a dog appeared and dragging at Dick Tozer's coat pulled him to the doorway of a burning building, scratching frantically at the door. Despite the danger, Dick Tozer forced his way in and, sure enough, there on the floor in the smoke lay a young girl. Dick carried her out, to the cheers of the crowd and the congratulations of the Prince of Wales, who was a keen amateur fireman (number 116) and often attended blazes in full uniform.

"Why not call him Chance – like the Watling Street fire-dog?" suggested the Prince. So Chance he became. Stranger still was the discovery that this Chance had, in fact, come from Peckham. He had arrived some time before, from nowhere, at the Adam and Eve stable run by horse master Thomas Tilling and made great friends with a horse called Bruce. Everyone loved his perpetually furrowed brow and popping eyes. But one day he vanished – just as he had come. No one knew where he went, until the Fleet Street fire.

Chance stayed on and Dick Tozer had a special thick collar engraved for him. It said: "Stop me not, but onward let me jog. For I am Chance, the London fireman's dog." He became a favourite on both sides of the river and was a regular at the Wednesday afternoon fire displays at the brigade's Southwark Bridge Road headquarters. The public bought tickets to see Chance and peer at the aristocrats, who came with the Prince to watch him in action at the show. On one un-rehearsed occasion the jetstream from the horse-drawn appliance, Fire Queen, removed the Royal top hat, which was retrieved by Chance from a puddle. On another, Chance climbed the fire escape ladder but could not get down and had to be rescued, to the delight of the spectators.

For many years Chance carried a charity collection box on his back. He died in harness. While leading men to a trapped and dying fireman he suffered internal injuries from a collapsing wall. Dick Tozer paid to have his body stuffed and he was then raffled. The funds raised were donated to widows and orphans.

SARAH WARDROPER

1812-1892

In 1854, at about the same time that Florence Nightingale was coping with the horror of caring for wounded soldiers in the Crimean War, ST THOMAS'S HOSPITAL in Southwark became a battleground of a different kind.

The Governors appointed a new matron, Mrs Sarah Wardroper. She was a controversial choice – a respectable, 42 year old, middle-class widow with four children, at a time when nursing was little better as a job for girls than a refuge from being a skivvy or a prostitute. There was no training for nurses; operations were often conducted on the ward, with no anaesthetic, and they coped with overcrowded, filthy conditions. Drunkenness became an all too common escape. Beer was the only beverage supplied, even to patients! It was common practice to put a patient into the same sheets used (and soiled) by the last occupant of the bed and mattresses were generally of flock and seldom, if ever, cleaned.

But Mrs Wardroper became the rock upon which her friend, Miss Nightingale, leant on her return; she was one of the great reforming matrons and later became principal of the first training centre for nurses in the country. One of Mrs Wardroper's most important innovations was to upgrade the status of her staff. She recruited specially chosen probationers of good class, who were subjected to a rigorous interview. Sisters were then promoted from the nursing staff, rather than from unqualified outsiders. She devoted herself to improving the quality of nurses and their working conditions.

When Miss Nightingale returned from the war she visited the hospital and found that Mrs Wardroper had "weeded out the inefficient, morally and technically; she had obtained better women as nurses; she had put her finger on some of the most flagrant blots, such as night nursing... but no training had yet been thought of..."

Her dedication impressed Florence Nightingale so greatly that she chose the Southwark hospital as the base for The Nightingale School for Nurses – established from a £45,000 fund, raised as a "thank you" for her courage and skill during the war.

It was Sarah Wardroper who made Florence Nightingale's dreams come true – not without a fight! Many doctors and surgeons resented and feared the possibility that girls could be trained medically and eventually threaten their own professional standing.

In 1860, at Florence Nightingale's request, Mrs Wardroper took over the management and training of the new Nightingale school. Her guide for probationers was that "you are required to be: sober, honest, truthful, trustworthy, punctual, quiet and orderly, cleanly and neat." Girls were also expected to learn a vastly greater range of skills than before including not only the dressing of wounds and the application of leeches but the administration of enemas for men and women, a knowledge of symptoms and basic cleanliness, and how to cook gruel, arrowroot and egg flip puddings.

In 1862 St Thomas's was finally uprooted after 600 years in Southwark to make way for a new railway line between London Bridge and Charing Cross. Its new, temporary home was a nightmare for Mrs Wardroper. The old Surrey Gardens Music Hall at Newington was a huge glass structure, part of which had been destroyed by fire and part of which had served as a zoo. The giraffe house became the cholera ward and the elephant house the dissecting room. The kitchen was converted into an operating room. Balconies were used for soiled linen and for the placing of portable lavatories. The main hall became the accommodation for some two hundred patients.

The fifteen probationers each had a room in the Nurses' Home and were supplied with books and even flowers by Miss Nightingale. Mrs Wardroper felt this was unnecessary indulgence. They wore brown

The old Surrey Gardens Music Hall, temporary home of St Thomas's Hospital.

dresses, white caps and aprons and were given an annual allowance of £10 during training. No longer were they expected to scour and clean but they were expected to study hard and to be neat, lady-like, vestal and above suspicion. Every month Mrs Wardroper prepared a report on "Personal Character and Acquirements" writing against each probationer's name "excellent", "good", "imperfect", or "0". Flirtation or "making eyes" was punished with instant dismissal and no Nightingale probationer was allowed to leave the home alone.

Mrs Wardroper "worked single handed, visiting the wards occasionally by night as well as by day. The stench was sometimes unbearable because windows were kept closed for fear of draughts."

Eventually a new site was found for St Thomas's on the riverside at Lambeth and in 1871, with Mrs Wardroper still at the helm, the hospital was moved to its present site by Westminster Bridge. She worked on tirelessly until she was seventy five years old, demanding of herself the standards she expected of her girls. The people of Southwark owe much to her devotion.

OCTAVIA HILL

1838-1912

Octavia Hill, SHORT, DUMPY AND DEEPLY RELIGIOUS, was a philanthropist and somewhat autocratic reformer in the grand Victorian tradition.

She believed fervently that by skilled and efficient management the poor could be given pleasant living surroundings which would encourage them to have a sense of self reliance and help them to stand on their own feet. Her goal was to create "well ordered, quiet little homes behind neat little doors." As a landlord she was strict, patronising and maternalistic. She did not believe in state subsidies and was a fierce opponent of the women's franchise movement.

At the age of 26, and with £3,000 provided by John Ruskin, she launched her career as a housing manager – her particular interest being the conversion and refurbishment of urban cottages and the provision of green spaces in many parts of London. She was totally against tenement blocks. Her reputation as an efficient but caring manager spread. As her philosophy that tenants, however poor, must pay their way produced a return of 5%, more and more owners of working class housing, such as The Ecclesiastical Commissioners, invited her to look after their properties. She helped her tenants find jobs, encouraged saving and gave advice wherever it was needed. Cabinet Ministers sought her counsel.

By 1884, she turned her attention towards the appalling conditions suffered by so many people in Southwark itself. She located "a waste, desolate place" in the area of The Mint. Here, on a one and a half acre site, at Red Cross Way, overlooked by the towering blocks of the Victoria Dwellings Company (which Miss Hill was also to manage) was a derelict paper factory. Piles of paper, blackened by fire, saturated by rain and smelling most unpleasantly had lain there for five years. Miss Hill immediately raised £2,500 to build six, 18th century-style, gabled, low rent cottages, with latticed windows, around a small garden and to convert a derelict building into a community centre.

In the summer of 1888 Octavia Hill's vision for Southwark came to fruition.

When the Archbishop of Canterbury opened the project on a sunny day in June, he waxed lyrical in his vision of the future. He described how, in an old Italian picture, he had seen "angels with wings walking among men and women, in a garden full of trees and flowers" and he hoped that this might prove possible even there.

The *South London Press* was equally ecstatic and described the event as "one of the greatest transformations that has taken place in South London within living memory. From narrow courts, loathsome dens and pestilential odours we are today introduced, as if by the wand of a magician, to wide streets, bright and wholesome habitations and sanitary surroundings of a high order". There was a fountain and a platform for entertainments. The hall itself housed a working men's club, a Cadets' Corps, a girls' club; concerts were planned as well as exhibitions and books to read.

Red Cross Cottages were one of Octavia Hill's many projects and her influence as a pioneer conservationist was to spread to cities all over Britain. In 1895 she co-founded the National Trust, now the largest private landowner in the country, and enthusiastically took selected tenants on outings to her beloved countryside.

Returning to Red Cross Cottages in May 1901, she wrote to her mother "the garden looked lovely: trees and creepers are growing, and the Good Shepherd gleamed out among them, as if watching over the glad crowd of happy children, who marched and danced and played in bright unconsciousness".

That year she took over the management of 50 houses in Southwark and 600 in Walworth. She persuaded the authorities to renovate properties and not demolish them when leases expired, or to build cottages rather than tenements if repair was not possible.

Octavia Hill retired, eventually, to her home in Crockham Hill in Kent, where she lived with a lady companion. With her masses of loose grey hair, her piercing eyes and formidable presence she commanded respect from all who met her. "I do love life and all it brings very deeply" she once said "and I should like to live as long too to see the progress of so many things I care for."

Sadly, it is hard to believe today that Red Cross Cottages and Red Cross Hall were once showplaces – a turning point – of which Southwark was justifiably proud. The little garden is once again threadbare and neglected, the fountains have gone. But Octavia Hill's belief that educated, prosperous people should work on a one-to-one basis with poorer individuals and their problems, that aid carried moral responsibilities for its recipients and that Acts of Parliament and relief systems alone could not work, is as controversial and relevant as it ever was.

BELLA OF THE RING

1877-1962

NOT FAR FROM THE SITE OF RENNIE'S MILL down Blackfriars Road – but 120 years later – the formidable Bella Burge was a phenomenon in the international boxing world. Between 1910 and 1940 she ruled "The Ring" with a rod of iron and "absolutely no hanky panky".

First with her husband, ex-heavy weight champion Dick Burge, and then, when he died in 1918, alone, she dominated the all-male rowdy, boxing crowd that packed the former chapel every night. They aimed to provide "fistic feasts for the cloth cap and muffler brigade."

South London was then the heartland of the boxing world. Bermondsey, in particular, produced six British champions between 1897-1914. The sport was a part of everyday life for most boys – it was a manly exercise.

Bella Burge was born Leah Belle Orchard in 1877, in America. From the age of four she longed to sing and act. By the time she was 12 she was in music hall in London. With her reddish hair and odd Cockney-American voice she was a huge success from the start. In 1901 she married the neat, fastidious boxer, Dick Burge. Later they together found a dirty, derelict building in Blackfriars Road but, partly because of its former life as a chapel, the owners refused Dick permission to convert it for such a hole-in-the-corner, unsalubrious sport as boxing. However, Bella, unbeknown to Dick, pleaded their case – and won.

Its almost circular shape with "no place for the devil to hide" made it an ideal boxing hall. A stray black kitten with a white ring round her throat provided the inspiration for the name and a home was found for her in "The Ring".

Bella hauled in tramps from the Embankment to help clear the rubble and, despite Dick's protests that "this is no place for a woman", she was present at the opening on 14 May 1910. Against his wishes and despite the notice at the entrance saying "no women admitted", she was there every evening from then on.

With her friend Marie Lloyd she installed a soup kitchen in the big open room at the back of the building, where together they ladled soup and gave free currant bread to poor children. Marie sang songs to cheer the poor: of course, their kindness helped improve the reputation of The Ring, which became a nursery for the whole of Britain's boxing talent.

The money rolled in and Dick lavished on Bella everything she wanted. Every day she drank half a pint of champagne with a knob of sugar, angostura bitters and lemon zest; she had a boat on the Thames and a fabulous wardrobe.

The Burges were the first to persuade a national paper – the *Daily Mirror* – to print a professional boxing picture but, even more exciting, Bella finally persuaded her husband to try to encourage more women spectators. He booked the romantic young French idol Georges Charpentier. In 1918 her beloved Dick succumbed to double pneumonia after a night spent helping bomb victims in the street. As he lay dying he asked Bella "Can you keep The Ring going on your own?" She was determined to try.

She made the boxers wear dressing gowns and smartened up the dressing rooms. She also introduced Sunday afternoon boxing so that the early rising men from the market could be there. She attracted a far smarter clientele; people like Dame Laura Knight, Douglas Fairbanks jnr and Marlene Dietrich came to The Ring, as did The Prince of Wales on an official visit.

Dick and Bella Burge.

In 1935 Bella celebrated The Ring's Grand Silver Jubilee with a glittering night of music hall and theatre. It was an emotional affair. But the world was changing around her and by 1939, with war threatened, audiences had dwindled. Bella began paying boxers from her savings until eventually she had nothing, and even pawned her jewellery. Friends begged her to stop and in October 1940 the future was taken out of her hands. A bomb demolished the old chapel and the new 25 year lease, waiting in her solicitor's office, was never signed. Bella continued to live quietly in her Bloomsbury flat until she died in September 1962.

And so, once more back to the river. The brewers, the brothel keepers, haddock smokers and the bone boilers have gone. Outwardly the borough has changed dramatically but Chaucer would still recognise the descendants of his "pilgrims" in the pubs, the parks, the alley-ways and courtyards. Back-packers and eager sight-seeing tourists mingle with residents old and new: some born here to "blush unseen". Together with other famous names like John Wesley, Sir Ernest Shackleton, P.G.Wodehouse, Tommy Steele, Max Bygraves, Norman Wisdom, Charlie Drake and Michael Caine they will all carry the colourful spirit of the borough forward to the future. Past and present, as literary historian Neville Coghill observed of Chaucer's pilgrims so long ago, they are all "sharply original: together they make a story."

It is the story of Southwark.

BOOKLIST

John Overs and King Olaf of Norway
Shepherd, C. W. *A Thousand Years of London Bridge*. John Baker, 1971.
An Antiquary, *Chronicles of London Bridge*. Smith Elder and Co., 1827.

John Taylor
Shepherd, C. W. *A Thousand Years of London Bridge*. John Baker, 1971.
Green, Martin *A Very Merry Wherry Voyage*. Dramatisation.
Pudney, John *Crossing London's River*. J. M. Dent and Sons Ltd., 1972.
Taylor, John *All the Works of John Taylor collected in one volume by the author*, 1630.

Madame Britannica Hollandia
Burford, E. J. *Queen of Bawds*. Neville Spearman, 1973.

John Rennie and Sir John Rennie
Reyburn, Wallace *Bridge Across the Atlantic*. Harrap, 1972.
Rennie, Sir John *Autobiography*. E and F. N. Spon, 1875.
The Dictionary of National Biography.

Sam Wanamaker
Day, Barry *This Wooden O*. Oberon Books, 1996.
South London Press
When, Where, Why and How it Happened. Readers Digest, 1993.

Mrs Thrale and Dr Johnson
Rendle and Norman *The Inns of Old Southwark*. Longmans, 1888.
Ingrams, Richard (ed) *Dr Johnson by Mrs Thrale*. Hogarth Press, 1984.

Dr Alfred Salter
Brockway, Fenner *Bermondsey Story. The life of Dr Alfred Salter*. Blackfriars Press, 1949.

Sir Marc Brunel and Isambard Kingdom Brunel
Mathewson, Andrew and Laval, Derek *Brunel's Tunnel*. Brunel exhibition, 1992.
Lampe, David *The Tunnel*. Harrap, 1963.
Trench, Richard and Hellman, Ellis *London Under London*. John Murray, 1984.

Prince Lee Boo
Peacock, Daniel J *Lee Boo of Belau*. South Sea Books, 1987.

Dr Harold Moody
Vaughan, David *A Negro Victory*. Independent Press, 1950.
Cuttings from the *South London Press*.
Beasley, John D. *The Story of Peckham and Nunhead*. London Borough of Southwark, 1999.

Edward Alleyn
Wraight, A. D. *Christopher Marlowe and Edward Alleyn*. Adam Hart, 1993.
Reid, Aileen and Maniura, Robert (ed) *Edward Alleyn*. Dulwich Picture Gallery, 1994.
Blanch, William Hartnell *Dulwich College and Edward Alleyn*. 1877.

John Ruskin
Tames, Richard *Dulwich and Camberwell Past, with Peckham*. Historical Publications, 1997.
Kemp, Wolfgang *A Life of John Ruskin*. Harper Collins. 1991.

Robert Browning
DeVane, William Clyde *A Browning Handbook*. G. Bell and Sons, 1955.
Thomas, Donald *Robert Browning*. Weidenfield and Nicolson, 1982.
Beasley, John D. *The Story of Peckham and Nunhead*. London Borough of Southwark, 1999.

Richard Cuming
Family papers in the Southwark Local Studies Library
Leaback, D. H. *Reweaving Rainbows*. Privately published, 2001.

Charles Chaplin
Haming, Peter (ed) *Charles Chaplin. A Centenary Celebration*. N. Foulsham & Co Ltd, 1989.
Charles Chaplin *My Autobiography*. Bodley Head, 1969.

John Harvard
Shelley, Henry C. *John Harvard and his Times*. Smith Elder and Co., 1907.
Boger, Mrs E. *Bygone Sourthwark*. Simpkins Marchall, Hamilton, Kent & Co., 1895.

Thomas Guy
Cameron, H. C. *Mr Guy's Hospital*. Longman, 1954.
Wilks, Samuel and Bettany, G. T. *A Biographical History of Guy's Hospital*.
Ward Lock, Bowden and Co, 1892.

Charles Dickens
Ackroyd, Peter *Dickens*. Sinclair Stevenson, 1990.

The East Family and The George Inn
East, John M *Neath the Mask*. George Allen and Unwin, 1967.

Captain Eyre Massey Shaw
Cox, Ronald *Oh, Capt, Shaw*. Victor Green, 1984.

The Fire Dogs of Southwark
Dudley, E *Chance and the Fire Horses*. Harvill Press, 1972.

Sarah Wardroper
Gordon, J. Elsie OBE *Distinguished British Nurses of the Past*. Midwife, Health Visitor and Community Nurse, 1975.
Parsons, F. G *The History of St Thomas's Hospital 1800-1900*. Methuen, 1936.
The Florence Nightingale Museum.
Leaflet; *Women, St Thomas's Hospital and The Old Operating Theatre*. The Old Operating Theatre and Herb Garrett, Tooley Street, Southwark.

Octavia Hill
Whelen, Robert (ed) *Octavia Hill and the Social Housing Debate*. IEA, 1998.
Darley, Gillian *Octavia Hill*. Constable, 1990.

Bella of The Ring
Bell, Leslie *Bella of Blackfriars*. Odhams, 1961.

INDEX

Alleyn, Edward	48-51
Alleyn's College of God's Gift	48-51
artists	
Ayres, Alice	5
Bailly, Harry	1
Bankside	24,28
Barclay Perkins Brewery	28-30
Barrett-Browning, Elizabeth	58
bear baiting	49
Bermondsey	31-35
Bermondsey Settlement	32
Blackfriars Bridge	20
Borough High Street	2, 66, 75
Borough, The	66-95
boxing	93-95
Braidwood, James	85
Brandon, Charles	5
brothels	16-19
Browning, Robert	56-58
Brunel, Sir Marc and Isambard Kingdom	36-39
Burge, Bella	93-95
Camberwell	56-58
Camberwell Green Congregational Church	46
Canterbury Tales	1
Chance, the fire dog	84-86
Chaplin, Charles	62-65
Chaucer, Geoffrey	1
Christ Church, Blackfriars Road	20
Cuming Museum	60-61
Cuming, John Brompton	60
Cuming, Henry Syer	61
Cuming, Richard	60-61

Denmark Hill	52
Dickens, Charles	72-74
Dickens, John	72
Doggett, Thomas	3
Dulwich	48-51
Dulwich College	48-51
East family	75-79
East London Railway Line	39
Elephant & Castle	62
Elephant and Castle Theatre	78
engineers	20-23, 36-39
fires and firefighting	80-86
food processing	5
The George Inn	75-79
Globe Theatre	24-27
Gordon Riots	30
Guy's Hospital	4, 31, 69-71
Guy, Thomas	69-71
Harvard, John	66-68
Harvard University	68
Herne Hill	54-55
health care	35, 44, 87
Hill, Octavia	52, 90-92
Hollandia, Britannica	16-19
hospitals	4, 31, 70-71, 87-89
housing	35, 90-92
Johnson, Dr Samuel	28-30
Keats, John	4
King's Bench Prison	37

Labour Party	32	St Olave's Church	11
League of Coloured Peoples	46	St Saviour's Church	9, 66
Lee Boo, Prince	40-42	St Thomas's Hospital	70-71, 87-89
Leverian Museum	61	Salter, Dr Alfred and Ada	31-35
London Bridge	9-10, 22-23, 37	Shakespeare, William	2
		Shaw, Eyre Massey	80
Marshalsea Prison	71-72	Southwark Bridge	22
Metropolitan Fire Brigade	80	Southwark Cathedral	9, 68
Mint, the	5, 45, 73-74, 82	South London Palace	78
Montpellier Theatre	64	Surrey Gardens Music Hall	88
Moody, Dr Harold	44-47		
		Tabard Inn	1
National Trust	92	Taylor, John	12-15
Newcomen, Elizabeth	5	Thames, River	12
Nightingale School for Nurses	88	Thames Tunnel	36-39
		theatres	24-27, 48, 62-65, 77-78
Olaf, King of Norway	10	Thrale, Henry & Mrs	28-30
O'Neil, Oona	65	Tooley Street fire	80, 85
Overs, John	8	Tranter, Mabel	45
Paris Garden, manor of	17	Wanamaker, Sam	24-27
Peckham	44-47	Wardroper, Sarah	87-89
prisons	37, 71-72	Waterloo Bridge	22
		Watermen and Lightermen, Company of	12-15
Queen's Head Inn	67	Woodward, Joan	49
		World War II	46
Red Cross Cottages and Way	90-92	writers	1-2, 52-55, 56-58, 72-74
Rennie, John and Sir John	20-23		
Ring, the	93-95	York Street Congregational Church	57
Rose Theatre	26		
Rotherhithe	36-42		
Ruskin, John	52-55, 90		

St Mary Overie, priory church of 8-9
   see also
   St Saviour's Church;
   Southwark Cathedral